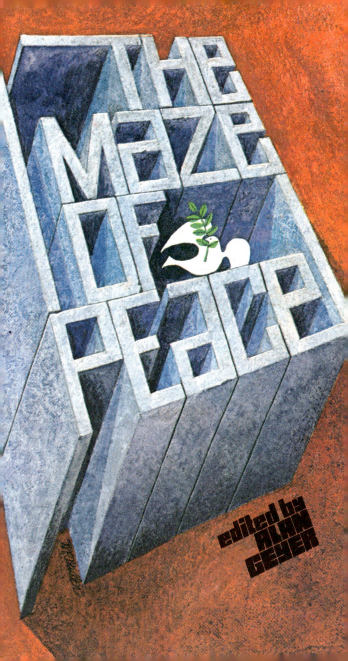

THE MAZE OF PEACE

edited by ALAN GEYER

THE MAZE OF PEACE:
Conflict and Reconciliation Among Nations

Alan Geyer, editor

"—if we really want to understand, we have to listen to the other side, even if it is painful."
—Christoph Schmauch, Chapter 4

The churches' seriousness about peace is being tested today as never before. Can the religious community work effectively in the arena of contending ideas and philosophies? Are we prepared to bring in-depth understanding to such complex fields as international development and trade, security and arms control and the structure of racial exploitation?

Young men and women committed to a peaceful world community will find these four contrasting reports on peace and reconciliation an important tool. The emphasis in the symposium is the urgent need for dialogue on issues as between what is biblically and theologically relevant and the explosive issues of political controversy, ideological struggle, religious tension, racial bitterness, economic disorder and the disarray of international institutions.

COVER DESIGN BY KEN MC MULLEN

THE MAZE OF PEACE

Conflict and
Reconciliation Among Nations

Edited by Alan Geyer

Friendship Press   New York

dedicated to

NANCY KATHRYN

PETER LINCOLN

DAVID CURTIS

PHILIP MARSHALL

four very young people
who have already borne very much
for the sake of peace
without quite knowing
what it is all about—
just like their father

All Bible quotations used in this book are from the Revised Standard Version, copyright, 1946 and 1952, by the Division of Christian Education of the National Council of the Churches of Christ in the United States of America.

Library of Congress Catalog Card Number: 68-589132

Copyright © 1969 by Friendship Press, Inc.
Printed in the United States of America.

Contents

Introduction

A chaplain at one of the largest American field hospitals in Vietnam was speaking of the impact of the war upon the sanity of the men compelled to fight in it. "We can't trouble them with moral questions out here," he said. "In Vietnam, you've got to stick your religion in your back pocket and forget about it, or you'd go crazy!"

This book may drive you crazy. It does not take a back pocket view of the relationship between religion and international conflict. It is concerned to trouble you with the most significant moral questions that can be raised about the meaning of reconciliation in a broken world.

The theme of reconciliation is woven through an admittedly coarse fabric of biblical dispute, political controversy, ideological struggle, religious tension, racial bitterness, economic disorder and diplomatic turbulence. It takes a religious

5

faith of the toughest possible fiber to get tangled up in the threads of all these issues without breaking. But then this book takes a tough view of what reconciliation is all about: it is engagement with the world at precisely the places where the tensions are most unbearable and most dangerous. The quest for peace leads through the maze of conflict.

You will not find this a completely unified, integrated book. The subject matter is many-sided. The four authors represent a variety of national and racial backgrounds, political viewpoints, theological interests, professional preoccupations. We would prefer that you think of the chapters that follow as a celebration of diversity rather than as an exposition of uniformity.

Yet we do share a large measure of agreement on the issues that must be confronted as men seek a peaceful world. Similarly, we share some agreement concerning what is required of the churches which must reconstruct themselves while they participate fully in the work of political reconciliation.

We are not professionals in Christian doctrine. Our use of terms like "a theology of peace" and "a doctrine of providence" may appear somewhat pretentious, especially to any systematic theologian who may happen upon these pages. Nevertheless, we ask indulgence in the hope that we may have something useful to say concerning the meaning of brokenness and reconciliation.

Christoph Schmauch is a pastor who serves

part-time on the staff of the Methodist Office for the United Nations. A German by birth and schooling, he is an officer of the Christian Peace Conference, which his father helped to establish.

Daisuke Kitagawa recently joined the staff of the Division of World Mission and Evangelism of the World Council of Churches in Geneva. He is the former executive secretary for the College and University Division of the Episcopal Church's Executive Council. He is a native of Japan.

Gerard N. T. Widdrington is director of United Nations Services for the Department of International Affairs of the National Council of the Churches of Christ in the U.S.A. An Englishman by birth and a Canadian by naturalization, Mr. Widdrington served for many years as an officer of the United Nations Secretariat.

Alan Geyer is editor of *The Christian Century*. A political scientist, Christian ethicist and former pastor, he came to his present position in 1968 from service as Director of International Relations for the United Church of Christ. An earlier book, *Piety and Politics* (1963), outlines a more theoretical approach to the themes of conflict and reconciliation in world politics.

Chapter I
Alan Geyer

The Maze of Conscience

On Christmas Eve in 1917, the war of attrition in France was halted for a few hours for singing Christmas carols. German trenches were close enough to British and American trenches for singing on each side to be heard on the other. "Silent Night" was rendered in English on the allied side; the response *"Stille Nacht"* came back from the German side. "Sleep in heavenly peace . . . *schlaf in himmlischer ruh'.* . . ."

It was a peculiarly poignant moment in Western history, this litany of sacred song between the trenches. All too soon these musical volleys would be replaced by the renewed exchange of artillery. Some of those who had sung together would be killed by their fellow carolers. They would be dispatched to "sleep in heavenly peace" in a manner that seemed to be a ghastly denial of the Christmas story.

But in that brief and holy lull on the Western front, Christian unity was celebrated above the hostilities of nations engaged in the cruelest war the world had known up to that time. In a sense, it was the last civil war to be fought within "Christendom," that historic unity of religion and civilization whose actual disunity had been the dominant historical fact for four centuries. To be sure, the next generation would witness another world war in which Christians would once again be enemies to one another. But World War II burst the boundaries of Christendom to become truly global: the Soviet Union, an antireligious state, and Shintoist Japan fractured the Christian lineup on both sides. And Nazism all but destroyed the church as a vital force in Germany.

The most somber fact in this book is that Christians, notwithstanding their gospel of love, peace and forgiveness, have never been wholly united among themselves, either in their understanding of the gospel's imperatives with regard to war and peace, or in their political and international action in the pursuit of peace (or justice, or freedom or any other goal).

It would be difficult enough for Christians to be an effective force for reconciliation in a broken world if, as a minority religion, Christianity could present a united front to the world. But Christians are so fragmented among themselves that they are part of the very brokenness they seek to overcome. The brokenness of the human family—nationally, racially, economically, ideologically, religiously—is the very condition that makes reconciliation meaningful. Conflicts among Christians themselves, as well as between Christians and others, thus form the maze within which we must discover what reconciliation is all about.

Conflicts among Christians over the issues of war and peace are not to be understood simply as perversions created in the modern period. Indeed, there has been a struggle on these issues within the soul of the church for its whole history. Nor is there any escape from this struggle by appealing to the testimony of Scripture alone. The New Testament is richly inspired in its passages on war and peace, but it cannot be invoked to settle the conflict for all time. Writing on the eve of World War II under the title *The New Testament Basis of Pacifism,* G.H.C. MacGregor was notably candid in acknowledging that

> Pacifists are perhaps too apt to assume without sufficient proof that Jesus' ethic is incontestably 'pacifist,' and that, even if so proved, He intended that pacifist ethic to be applied to the wider sphere of social and national politics. Our opponents still more light-heartedly deny this, with an even greater lack of demonstration.[1]

Whether pacifists or nonpacifists are actually more guilty in their misunderstanding, misuse and manipulation of the Scriptures need not concern us here: the author of this chapter happens to be a nonpacifist who assumes that, in the three decades since MacGregor's book was published, the traditional boundaries between pacifists and nonpacifists have been greatly altered by the impact of military technology and the revolutionary struggles of the "Third World" of Asia, Africa and Latin America. It remains true that biblical proof texting about the issues of war and peace is a game that no Christian individual or group can win in any permanent or absolute sense. This seeming limitation of the Bible could be regarded as a tragic disappointment. If only the charter of our faith had given us clear and unarguable instructions, blueprints for building a peaceful world—what a great book it would really be!

But the Bible is not a volume of blueprints. Thank God it is not! We must learn to be grateful for the fact that the Scriptures speak in dialogue between God and men, and among men themselves, and that the religious struggle is open and endless. Jesus' own mission was a perennial challenge to the notion that the interpretations of justice and righteousness could be frozen, whether in commandments, laws or rituals. The faith that we see in Jesus and learn from Jesus is a *quest*. The truly ethical life is a seeking, asking, knocking, struggling life in which the most important things never lose the dimensions of miracle and mystery. The meaning of reconciliation remains a struggle within the soul of the most consecrated ambassador for Christ. It lies not only in our having conflicting ideological views in any present situation. It is also a struggle that begins in the

11

most honest scrutiny of the Scriptures, where living men sought to be obedient to a living God.

Both the pacifist, who repudiates war and refuses participation in it, and the nonpacifist can—and must—find instruction in the biblical dialogue on the meaning of reconciliation. "You shall not kill" and "Love your enemies" remain important texts for both the pacifist and the nonpacifist to reckon with. They are not the only texts, however, that give some content to the Christian witness. "I have not come to bring peace, but a sword" is another, and very difficult, text. "Obey your leaders and submit to them" is another, as is "making peace by the blood of his cross."

If these few pages cannot pretend to begin to untangle the biblical and theological dilemmas associated with the issues of war and peace, they at least can pose some of the perennial questions with which a theology of peacemaking must grapple. Or, to put it more constructively, we may identify a cluster of doctrines or ideas that must be incorporated into an adequate interpretation of the message of reconciliation as addressed to the problem of international conflict. Somewhat tentatively, let us specify ten such doctrines that can and must draw upon biblical sources of insight and inspiration:

1. *A doctrine of providence* that confronts the question of God's action in history as Creator, Judge and Redeemer of all men and all nations;

2. *A doctrine of love* that confronts the ques-

tion of the relationship of love to justice, order, freedom and welfare as goals of the political community;

3. *A doctrine of authority* that confronts the question of the place coercive law enforcement has in the fullest possible expression of love and justice in human society, and when or whether civil disobedience can be morally justified;

4. *A doctrine of war* that confronts the question of war as an instrument of love or justice and, if it is, how the means of waging war can be morally controlled;

5. *A doctrine of violence* that confronts the question of the legitimacy of violence and what place must be given to a philosophy or strategy of nonviolence;

6. *A doctrine of revolution* that confronts the question of the requirements of love or justice for radical changes in the powers of government, and the legitimate means of bringing about such changes;

7. *A doctrine of the enemy* that confronts the question of the human claims, if any, of the military and civilian forces of opposed nations, and of whether God's judgment is active through enemies as well as allies;

8. *A doctrine of interdependence* that confronts the question of the forms of international government and action that are required by the common needs of nations for security and welfare, and for the peaceful resolution of their conflicts with one another;

13

9. *A doctrine of sacrifice* that confronts the question of the necessity of renunciation and suffering for the sake of other people and for the common quest for peace;

10. *A doctrine of mission* that confronts the question of the special work and witness of the church as a universal fellowship touching all national and racial groups.

These ten doctrines, or fundamental ideas about which questions must be raised, are not to be skipped over lightly in the casual reading of this book. They are not simply relics of the biblical past. They provide the active agenda for Christian relevance for the remainder of the twentieth century. They are great pivot points for unending study, thinking, discussion, action. They must be returned to again and again as an index to the chapters that the churches, and you as an individual, are writing as you try to bring theology, ethics, and political philosophy together in your own experience.

You cannot write these chapters alone. As other chapters in this book will make clear, you must pursue these questions in company with Christians and non-Christians of other nations, races and ideologies, who will show you truths that you cannot learn in separation from them, and distortions of the truth that deserve the most intent examination by your own mind.

A theology of peace is thus not a simple topic of one or two dimensions. It is not a subject that can be cut off from the fullness of the Christian faith in all realms of personal and corporate life. You must expect to have the imagination and discipline of your mind taxed severely by any meaningful commitment as a peacemaker. This is not to put the highest possible value upon abstract intellectualizing about peace: it is to warn you about the opposite peril of reducing the hard work of reconciliation to "goodwill" or simple moral passion. We have much anti-intellectualism to live down in both the churches and the politics of America, as Richard Hofstadter has reminded us in his Pulitzer Prize book.[2]

As the agenda of international affairs has become increasingly flooded with technological considerations and with the complexities of interdependence, the will to peace on the part of some souls has been crippled by a nostalgia for an earlier time and a more innocent morality. After hearing some of the frustrating dilemmas and ambiguities of international conflict discussed at the Inter-Religious Conference on Peace in Washington in March, 1966, one delegate rose in conspicuous impatience and proposed that the conference not bother about all those things but just declare itself "in favor of peace pure and simple." (His proposal was warmly applauded by some of his weary colleagues.) The churches' seriousness about peace is being tested as never before by their willingness to dig as deeply as possible into the complexities of international development and trade, security and arms control, and the structures of racial exploitation, and by their

15

willingness to offer themselves as meeting grounds for dialogue among contending philosophies. A mature theology of peace is grounded in the depth and breadth of reconciliation in the common life of men and nations.

Throughout Christian history, contradictory answers have been given to these perennial theological questions as well as to the particular political issues that Christians have confronted in the past. It is probably futile and perhaps even undesirable to hope that these contradictions will ever cease. They represent cleavages among thoughtful people, who have been engaged in lifelong wrestling over the full range of theological questions we have raised. They also represent immature convictions among those who have fixations on just one or two of these questions.

We cannot say—we have no right to say—with absolute confidence what *the* Christian position is: pacifist or nonpacifist, authoritarian or revolutionary, world federalist or nationalist. We can say —indeed we must say—that a thoroughgoing theology of peace must represent the grappling of the gospel of reconciliation with the meaning of providence, love and justice, authority, war, violence, revolution, enmity, interdependence, sacrifice and mission.

When the early church was a persecuted minority within the pagan Roman Empire, it nurtured a witness of pacifism and conscientious objection to military service.

When persecution gave way to the acceptance

16

and even the establishment of Christianity, the church developed a doctrine of "the just war" by which certain wars were justified as expressions of the rights and obligations of rulers, while other wars were to be rejected as unjust.

When political and religious authority combined under the medieval papacy, the church fostered crusades against the infidels that not only justified its decision to go to war but also declared the warfare itself to be a holy cause and a path to sainthood.

These three expressions of Christian conscience—pacifism, the just war and the crusade—have all continued to claim the conscience of Christians down through the centuries and into our own era, with contemporary variations.

Christian discussion of nuclear weapons and of revolutionary warfare (the latter is most frequently discussed in the context of Southeast Asia) during the 1960's was marked by a revival of interest in the "just war" doctrine. It has also recently been claimed by some scholars, such as Ralph Potter of Harvard, that all Christians have a "just war" doctrine whether they acknowledge it or not. Let us recall the principal criteria of justice that this doctrine elaborated, from St. Ambrose and St. Augustine in the early church through St. Thomas Aquinas and his followers in subsequent centuries.

1. A decision to wage war may only be a *last resort*. Every reasonable opportunity for peaceful settlement of the dispute must be pursued be-

fore deliberate violence may be sanctioned. Consistent with this criterion is the notion that every reasonable opportunity for a negotiated settlement of the war must be seized.

2. A decision to wage war may only be made by *legitimate authority:* a prince or magistrate, in ancient usage, or a proper decision of a sovereign government or international organization of legal competence, in modern usage. (This criterion is admittedly in present trouble because of undeclared wars and warfare waged by revolutionary movements seeking social justice.)

3. The object of a war must proceed from a *just cause*—that is, to vindicate justice itself. Augustine said: "Those wars may be defined as just which avenge injuries." Such injuries include not only an attack on the very existence of a state, but also such things as a failure to make amends or a refusal to grant passage. (Augustine tended to take for granted the notion that justice would lie wholly on one side in such a conflict. A mutuality of guilt and blame is very problematical for a "just war" doctrine, or for any doctrine of war.)

4. The war must be waged with a *just intent*. That intent is not self-aggrandizement or victory in any absolutely destructive sense, but rather the restoration of peace with justice. "Even in the course of war you should cherish the spirit of a peacemaker," Augustine said.

5. The war must be waged under the control of a *loving disposition*. Justice must be controlled by love. "No one indeed is fit to inflict punishment

save the one who has first overcome hate in his heart." This inward disposition often requires a mournful mood. The public official may be required by his office to participate in killing or even torture, but he will do so knowing that innocent people are often the victims of his own actions. "He will take his seat and cry 'From my necessities deliver Thou me!'"

6. The war must be executed through *just conduct*. This is a restraint upon the means of warfare. Even the enemy has human rights that must be respected. In particular, this criterion affirms the principle of *noncombatant immunity*, which Paul Ramsey of Princeton and others have declared to be, in its intention, the very heart of the "just war" doctrine. (There has been much sophisticated discussion by Ramsey and others of the morality of the unintentional killing of noncombatants, particularly with regard to weapons of counterinsurgency.) This criterion is also a repudiation of massacres, atrocities, reprisals, looting and wanton violence.

7. The damages inflicted must be guided by the norm of *proportionality*. Small-scale injuries should not be avenged by large-scale devastation and death. Justice is violated when loss of life and property increases without clear evidence that the original intent of the warfare is being respected and realized. This criterion is a reproach to the apparent senselessness of much, if not all, massive violence.

8. Wars should not be undertaken or continued

without a *reasonable prospect of success*. It is no act of justice to submit a people to the suffering and sacrifice of war if that war appears destined to fail in its object.

Altogether, these criteria of the traditional "just war" doctrine represent a rational set of questions with which to probe the morality of any present or contemplated war or act of war.

The twentieth century concept of total war raises a host of new questions about these traditional criteria, as well as the traditional formulations of the pacifist and the crusader.

On one hand is the opinion that pacifism has become irrelevant for three reasons: Modern warfare, in which personal witness becomes invisible to the enemy, has an impersonal, long-range character. Totalitarian dangers posed by nazism, fascism and communism raise the threat of extinction of faith and freedom. Violence on a wide scale is inevitable in the revolutionary postcolonial struggle for justice and nationhood in Asia, Africa and Latin America.

On the other hand is the opinion that the catastrophic qualities of nuclear bombs and missiles are so ghastly and inhuman that it is impossible to view modern warfare in terms of the "just war" tradition. There is no justice that can be served by the annihilation of tens or hundreds of millions of people, the resulting social and political chaos among the "survivors who would envy the dead" (the phrase is Nikita Khrushchev's) and the long-term effects of fallout and genetic damage.

To those who continue to appeal to the crusade tradition (as in "Christian Anti-Communist Crusade"), it should be recalled that the religious and ideological wars of past centuries have been the most brutal of all. With the weapons now at the disposal of great powers, there can be no more thought of seeking total victory or unconditional surrender or the extinction of an adversary. Peaceful coexistence has become an absolute requirement for human survival.

Yet the three traditions continue.

The pacifist sees in the mass destruction of modern wars and the costliness of the military establishment, a final historic vindication of his moral and theological repudiation of war and military service.

The adherent to "just war" doctrine sees it as the only politically feasible restraint upon nuclear weapons, and makes an earnest distinction between *possession* of nuclear weapons for reasons of deterrence and the *use* of them. He also claims that his doctrine gives relevant guidance for facing the inevitable violence of revolutionary warfare. He may appeal to the war in Vietnam as either a case of justifiable but limited war, or as an unjust war that he repudiates on nonpacifist grounds.

The crusader continues to see in one "ism" or another the greatest possible evil, and is willing to discount the casualties and material consequences of risking a nuclear war by appealing to "spiritual values" that he believes transcend hu-

21

man survival. "Better dead than Red," he says.

Reconciliation among these righteous advocates remains one of the most demanding and perplexing tasks for the life and mission of the church.

The escalation of the Vietnam war beginning in 1965 led to an unprecedented degree of moral intensity in public debate. It is not too much to say that the religious community, apart from the pacifists, had been overwhelmingly convinced of the justice and righteousness of American war aims in 1917-1918, 1941-1945 and in the Korean War. "God Bless America!" had captured the spiritual mood of the nation during those conflicts.

The situation in Vietnam drastically changed this moral lineup. Pacifists found themselves supported by a new company that included distinguished generals (Ridgeway, Gavin, Shoup), many of the "political realists" of the academic and religious worlds, who formerly had rationalized United States defense policy and criticized pacifists (Hans Morgenthau, George F. Kennan, Reinhold Niebuhr, John C. Bennett), prominent senators (J.W. Fulbright, the late Robert Kennedy, Eugene McCarthy, Joseph Clark, Wayne Morse, Thruston Morton, Clifford Case) and powerful voices of the press establishment (*The New York Times* and Walter Lippman). As casualties mounted on all sides and the villages and countryside of Vietnam were subjected to increasing devastation, as the political and moral weaknesses of the Saigon government were exposed, as the increasing isolation of the United

States from other nations on all continents became apparent, as the costs of the war mounted at the expense of the War on Poverty both in American cities and in the developing countries, as the inequities of the prevailing Selective Service System burst upon the public conscience, as television brought the tragedies and cruelties of the war as well as protest demonstrations into the living rooms and bedrooms of America, the churches were burdened with a moral struggle that they were ill-equipped to handle.

Dissension on the fundamental issues of the war itself, in the very midst of that war, was something new.

The solidarity of religious leadership and of the administration-religious coalition that had been forged in the civil rights struggle of the early 1960's (and in many years of religious support for the administration on United Nations and foreign aid issues) was shattered.

Religious leaders became involved in a jet age traffic pattern that took them to Saigon, Hanoi, Tokyo, Paris, Prague, the Vatican and other international vantage points for the Vietnam war.

There was another traffic pattern on the home front: dissenters were in the streets, in and out of police stations, jails and courts.

On the more reflective side, most if not all of the ten doctrines we have mentioned were opened up for reexamination. Looking back over that list, we may note particularly that:

1. with regard to a *doctrine of providence,* it

was repeatedly charged that the American nation had become arrogant and pretentious in the use of its power ("playing God" or "playing global policeman"), and had lost the sense of being under transcendent judgment.

2. with regard to a *doctrine of war*, the classical "just war" theory was not only invoked to defend the Vietnam war's presumed justice but also to protest its presumed injustice.

3. with regard to a *doctrine of authority*, there were allegations that the Vietnam war was unconstitutional and as a result there were increasing numbers of appeals to the doctrine of civil disobedience for the sake of a "higher law" of human obligation.

4. with regard to a *doctrine of revolution*, it was charged that American policy had actually become counterrevolutionary, and that the prevailing public philosophy had lost any authentic notion of revolutionary justice. Yet United States policy continued to call its program "revolutionary development" in South Vietnam.

5. with regard to a *doctrine of the enemy*, there is among Christians a remarkable sense of recovery of a lost article of faith and rediscovery of the humanity of the other side.

We can't deal with all these points here, but three themes call for extended comment.

Selective Objectors

Within the past three years we have witnessed a new form of the old "just war" doctrine: *selec-*

tive conscientious objection. The selective objector is a nonpacifist who believes that a particular war (such as the Vietnam war) is unjust, and that he cannot conscientiously serve in it. He is likely to appeal to the findings of the Nuremberg trials and to the American assumption that there is a higher law of conscience to which some officials of Nazi Germany should have been responsive. He repudiates unquestioning obedience to authority in matters involving crimes against humanity itself.

Thousands of draft-age Americans have claimed that the Vietnam war is repugnant to their consciences and a crime against humanity. Some of them are familiar with the traditional criteria of the "just war" doctrine and have argued (as has Senator Eugene McCarthy, a lay Catholic theologian of considerable sophistication) that the criterion of *proportionality* was violated in Vietnam beginning in 1965 or 1966: the war was leading to death and destruction on a scale that was beyond any legitimacy in terms of the original rationale for American intervention. Others have appealed to what they regard as violations of the emphasis that the "just war" doctrine places upon *legitimate authority* (the Congress has not been asked to declare a state of war nor has the United Nations sanctioned United States intervention), or upon *just intent* (the protection of peace and self-determination in Southeast Asia has, it is claimed, served as a rhetorical excuse for retaining an anti-Chinese military presence on the Asian mainland), or upon *just con-duct* (the war has been marked by terror and tor-ture and the mass killing of civilians on all sides), or upon *last resort* (opportunities for negotiations or other forms of political settlement may have been neglected by the United States).

The position of selective objection is thus far without legal status within the provisions of Se-lective Service law. Only the pacifist is accorded the legal privilege (it is not yet affirmed as a *right*) of exemption and alternative service on the grounds of conscientious objection. The un-willingness of Congress to extend the provisions of alternative service to nonpacifist objectors, com-bined with Selective Service Director General Lewis B. Hershey's frequent expressions of con-tempt for political protest and the inequitable ad-ministration of present laws, have led to an in-creasingly ugly crisis over the draft.

The General Board of the National Council of Churches and the General Synod of the United Church of Christ both adopted policy statements during 1967, recognizing the moral integrity of selective conscientious objection as a "third op-tion" and urging Congress to amend the Selective Service Act to provide alternative service for se-lective objectors. The United Church of Christ pronouncement is notable in its reflection of tra-ditional "just war" criteria. Its third and fourth paragraphs read:

WHEREAS there are, both within and without

the fellowship of the United Church of Christ, persons who do not renounce the use of military force as in itself inconsistent with their understanding of their moral obligation but at the same time are persuaded on grounds of conscience that war under given particular circumstances is wrong and that, therefore, they cannot under these conditions engage in military service; and WHEREAS they are led to this conclusion by such factors as their belief that the nation has not adequately explored peaceful means of settling international disputes, that the aims of a particular war cannot be ethically justified, that the means used for the prosecution of the war violate the moral standards which should prevail among nations, or that the probable evil consequences would greatly outweigh the hoped for good. . . .

The selective objector issue is not simply a new challenge to draft classification: it is a challenge that has arisen from within the military community itself. In a Federal District Court in Denver, in April, 1967, Captain Dale E. Noyd, a fighter pilot (described by the former Air Force Academy chaplain as "totally and thoroughly sincere" and having "more integrity than any person I've ever met") explained that he was compelled by conscience to say "no" to assignment in Vietnam. He is not a pacifist, and he does not object to continuing military service somewhere else. "The basis of my faith, beliefs and values," he said, "is humanism. This essentially means respect and love for man, faith in his inherent goodness and

27

perfectability and confidence in his capability to ameliorate some of the banes of the human condition." Captain Noyd lost his case in court and was later courtmartialed for refusing to train pilots for the Vietnam War.

A Theology of Revolution

There is a new mood of revolutionary discontent among many thousands of Americans, especially but not exclusively among young people. Dissent over the war, the draft and the military establishment has combined with moral outrage over poverty and racism in our cities and in the underdeveloped countries to generate this new mood. The New Left, Black Power, *Ramparts*, the Resistance, the "dump-Johnson" movements and the hippie colonies are some of the varied and spectacular symbols of this mood, but this mood is part of a much more extensive and less articulate feeling of malaise within the political and religious mainstream. There is a pervasive anxiety over the health of our institutions and a growing disaffection with established leadership and authority. Whether this mood can find constructive political expression, philosophical clarity, or religious guidance is a question that looms very large. We must also ask whether with all our wealth and power as a nation we have become so counter-revolutionary that we can only, as economist Robert Heilbroner contends, react negatively to these phenomena of revolutionary discontent.

When, where and how is it possible, or necessary, for a Christian to become a revolutionary? When is revolution the precondition of reconciliation?

It is the judgment of some Christians in Asia that there can be no ultimate reconciliation without a positive participation in present revolution. A landmark in revolutionary theology was a 1959 report of the first Assembly of the East Asia Christian Conference at Kuala Lumpur:

> The Church must endeavour to discern how Christ is at work in the revolutions of contemporary Asia: releasing new creative forces, judging idolatry and false gods, leading peoples to a decision for or against him, and gathering to himself those who respond in faith to him, in order to send them back into the world to be witnesses to his Kingship. The Church must not only discern Christ in the changing life but be there in it, responding to him and making his presence and lordship known.

This readiness to accept the dynamism of emerging nations not only as a grim secular necessity but also as a human participation in the work of Christ combines a doctrine of revolution with a doctrine of providence. The American presence in Southeast Asia has been plagued by an almost unbelievable poverty of understanding of revolution in either secular or religious terms. More in sadness than in anger, a high-ranking Vietnamese official shared this judgment with the writer during a visit in Saigon: "We are supposed to be carrying on a progam in 'revolutionary development' here, but neither your government nor my government seems to have any meaningful philosophy, any coherent ideas, any strategic doctrine of what a revolution is all about." There has been an American preoccupation with military hardware and with dollar aid to the exclusion of the pursuit of social justice for the disinherited. There has been such a chronic default in getting to the bottom of the revolutionary situation politically because of a fixation on preserving the stability of the regime, *any* Saigon regime, that the long-term prospects for stability itself have been undermined by unrelieved injustice.

This is a notorious weakness in regimes beset by revolution: the more frantic their quest for order and security to the neglect of social justice, the more certain it becomes that the revolution will erupt in violence and shatter the regime itself. A doctrine of violence becomes connected with a doctrine of revolution.

A theology of revolution cannot pretend that violence, inequality, coercion, compromise or any of the other raw materials of political life can be banished. Violence may not be more immoral than all forms of nonviolence. In fact, violence is not a very simple thing to define. There is such a thing as the "violence of order": the coercive stifling of protest and dissent. Moral responsibility for violence ultimately may not belong to those who first resort to it in overt physical forms: it may belong to the proudest patrons of law and order who have never learned that "justice delayed is justice denied." Reinhold Niebuhr shocked our bourgeois fixations on law and order and exposed our fears of anarchy and conflict by declaring: "If a season of violence can establish a just social system and can create the possibilities of its preservation, there is no purely ethical ground upon which it can be ruled out." Niebuhr insists (as did Abraham Lincoln) that violence, bitter as it may be, serves at times as an instrument of a higher justice and ultimate reconciliation. There is no harder question for faith and ethics than this: when is violence an instrument of Providence?

American Christians have been slow to respond to the historical meaning of revolutionary turbulence in Latin America. President John Kennedy warned on the first anniversary of the Alliance for Progress in March 1962:

> Those who possess wealth and power in poor nations must accept their responsibilities. . . .
> Those who make peaceful revolution impossible will make violent revolution inevitable.

But many noncommunists in Latin American lands had already dubbed the Alliance for Progress "the Castro Plan" because it seemed to them that it required the shock of Cuba's turn to Marxism-Leninism to arouse the United States from its lethargic attitude toward Latin America. Some progressive Christians agreed with these Latin Americans, even though they were well aware of the threats posed by the Marxist left. Theirs, of

31

course, is not really a new theology of international politics: that God should use even a Castro for his own mysterious purposes is pure Old Testament prophecy in the same mode as Yahweh's dealing with his chosen people through their enemies. And so within the context of a theology of revolution we may connect another pair of doctrines on our list: a doctrine of the enemy and a doctrine of providence. Sometimes God works his judgment upon us through the very enemy who is set against us. This may even be a very harsh and disastrous judgment on us: reconciliation may be terribly costly.

A theology of revolution must not, of course, be regarded as an uncritical endorsement of social upheaval in any and every setting. It is at least as important to resist the injustices of all revolutions as it is to exhort people to enlist in revolutionary movements. Revolution as such is never to be idolized as God's chosen instrument of political justice. A theology of revolution must not become an idolatry of revolution. Such a sentimental faith offers no improvement over the idolatry of the status quo, and can be as heedless of the requirements of reconciliation as any entrenched tyranny. There is no automatic preference for either change or stability in Christian morality. Revolution may be the most redemptive expression of ethical action in given circumstances, but it also may and will give vent to the most immature and irresponsible passions, or serve as the tool of pretentious interests and

narrow ambitions or issue in outrageous and re-
morseless cruelty. Richard Shaull writes:

> Revolution is a highly ambiguous phenomenon.
> It represents a passion for justice and for the
> liberation of the oppressed, but it also releases
> great forces of destruction and leads to new
> forms of injustice. Vast numbers of men and
> women have struggled and sacrificed their lives
> for the sake of a new society; all too often, the
> order that is established after the revolution has
> spent itself is not very different from the previ-
> ous one. Movements that succeed in awakening
> the masses and invite them to participate in the
> use of public power often lead to destructive
> fanaticism and end up by depriving them of
> power.[3]

All revolutions overreach themselves in their
self-righteousness. Legitimate grievances mix
with romantic adventurism, messianic ego involvement and styles of action that are
grotesquely disproportionate to the evils to be
overcome. The fabric of law and order in a liberal political system, whatever its faults, is likely
to be a hard won achievement of generations.
Those for whom civil liberties are most precious
must therefore make every possible effort to enhance the opportunities for intergroup relations,
nonviolent protest and the correction of injustice
if they would safeguard those liberties for themselves. The first line of defense for political freedom is neither guns nor courtrooms: it is the unrelenting pursuit of social justice for the disenher-

ited. This is the hard lesson that governments, universities and churches are painfully learning in this revolutionary season.

But those tempted to resort to the violent overthrow of established constitutional governments for inadequate reasons or out of an impatience with the democratic process are likely to produce more injustice than justice, and must expect to bear the force and the penalties of the law for their actions. No government can permit every movement or self-appointed messiah to shatter the integrity of the civil community, and with it the rights and liberties of its citizens. A government of laws and not of men is no mere bourgeois ideal, as some pretended radicals would have it: it is a social necessity for any political system committed to the humane vision of a just society. Some nihilists on the radical left have much more in common with the vigilantes and fascists of earlier generations than they care to admit.

Any Christian participation in revolution must be guided by an awareness of the spiritual arrogance and brutality that are all too frequently unleashed by revolutionary movements. It must also be guided by a profound sense of tragedy over the necessity of resorting to revolutionary methods, by an unrelenting effort to mitigate the excesses of revolutionary action (such as vandalism, terror, torture), by an alertness to every possibility of achieving just goals through nonviolent means and by continuing supplication for God's mercy and forgiveness for the wrongs in which one is implicated. It means not presuming too much about one's own revolution as an instrument of judgment, but rather accepting an unceasing submission to divine judgment.

The more conspiratorial and violent styles of revolutionary action are at best the last resort for a Christian. A case can be made for revolution when a colonial power deprives the people of another race of their freedom to express their own nationhood, and represses even nonviolent nationalist movements with legal harassment, imprisonment and execution. (Some of the most impressive Christian leaders of our time are nationalist revolutionaries in various parts of southern Africa.) A case can be made for revolution when a tiny oligarchy of ruling families own both the government and the land and controls the army and the church; when it uses a democratic constitution as fraudulent advertising for a system of mass exploitation, and brutally resists any effort to expose, discuss or reform the system. A case can be made for revolution when a government, economy and educational system are exclusively controlled by one racial or religious group to the systematic oppression of another racial or religious group within the same society. A case can be made for revolution when a dictatorship or alien military force tyrannizes the political rights of a people, destroys their cultural heritage and creativity, suppresses their religious heritage, liquidates individuals and groups and causes mass destruction and suffering.

To say, as we have here, that a case can be made for revolution in a particular situation is to speak primarily of a just cause and just intent—to refer again to two criteria of the traditional "just war" theory. But, as with the application of that theory to conventional warfare, there are other questions that must be raised, such as the immunity of more or less innocent people, the proportion of devastation and death in relation to the injustice to be overcome and the reasonable prospects for success in what could become a futile, senseless and cruel gesture. In both Eastern Europe and the United States there are obvious injustices that might seem to call for violent upheaval—but in both settings, alternative courses of action have been available, and the prospects for success on the part of a violent uprising are doubtful. The murders of Martin Luther King and Robert Kennedy may have caused an already faltering faith in nonviolence to be shattered at a critically important moment in American events, but they hardly increased the prospects for success of a strategy of violent black warfare. The sensitive Christian conscience must face these dilemmas before deciding to go underground, or to join a movement that some students have called "Guerrillas for Jesus."

A theology of revolution must keep the human values of justice and order in responsible tension with one another. A doctrine of interdependence will remind the Christian that the satisfaction of moral outrage as a revolutionary goal must be chastened by the need of all men for common institutions that enhance their mutual security. The legitimacy of revolution must finally be vindicated by its being grounded in the hope for reconciliation. In political terms, the Christian must know that the maintenance of international equilibrium—of a balance of power—may claim his peacemaking energies more decisively than the vindication of grievances.

A Theology of the Enemy

We have seen that within the context of revolution, God's justice may become active through those whom we regard as our enemies. Let us now look more directly at this fact of enmity among God's peoples.

There are some very brave young Vietnam Christian Service workers in hospitals and clinics who have been looking desperately for new ways to witness to what we have together called a theology of the enemy. They are keenly troubled that Vietnam Christian Service is largely restricted to one side in the war, and to areas of United States military security. They are willing to risk their lives for the sake of establishing new ministries to human need in insecure areas, or in areas dominated by the Viet Cong. They also know that some of their present ministry includes individuals and families who come to them from the other side. Here are Christian young people living on the newest frontiers of our faith, but they are new only because we have been so slow to re-

construct the gospel's own theology of the enemy
that has been there in the book for 2,000 years.
Until now we have dismissed it as a dead letter.

An even more dramatic, if more problematical,
witness to human need on the other side was the
voyage of the little ship *Phoenix*. She was loaded
with medical supplies from a group of American
Quakers, and sailed through war zones into
Haiphong harbor. The human equation in this
daring feat may not be much different from that
celebrated in a news release from Saigon that
proudly told of United States Army doctors who
knew that some cases they treated were known
or believed to be Viet Cong, but who refused to
discriminate in their compassion.

We have, however, a constitutional prohibition
against "giving aid and comfort to the enemies of
the United States," which action is described as
"treason." Here is an apparent conflict between
our highest written law and a new humanism that
is reaching out beyond all boundaries. Let us not
say that dialogue or coexistence across the chasms
of ideological conflict is simply a matter of words.
In Southeast Asia and similar areas of violence, it
may take many deeds, *acts* of uncommon
heroism and mercy by individuals and by governments, before human community can be restored.
The costliness of reconciliation in terms of suffering freely chosen and patiently endured to
the point of death is hardly a new idea: it is
at the very core of what the gospel is all about.

These imperatives of suffering and sacrifice as

inescapable burdens of the ministry of reconciliation are fundamental to a pacifist theology of peace. But they belong no less to the theology of those nonpacifists who regard the ministry of reconciliation as their touchstone in the issues of war and peace. They are enjoined by the "just war" doctrine's requirement that justice must be controlled by love even in the waging of war.

The overcoming of hatred for the enemy in one's own heart is an Augustinian (and biblical) command that is present in all political and military circumstances. This does not mean ignoring or minimizing the inhuman practices on the other side, or refusing to resist them: it does mean keeping alive the vivid sense of the common humanity on all sides, and an acknowledgement of one's own guilt. Repentance is at the very core of reconciliation in New Testament teaching. Translating repentance into political responsibility is never an easy task, but the Christian confesses that it must be done.[4]

Not long ago, the writer found himself in Prague, Czechoslovakia, meeting with the Ambassador of North Vietnam and the press representative of the National Liberation Front. It is a strange sensation, this meeting of the enemy in the middle of a war. Much of what they had to say invited skepticism. They certainly gave me no real signs of hope that the war could be ended soon. Indeed, I had been much more skeptical than some of my friends about the possibilities of "peace feelers" coming from such conversations,

not to mention the fact that the original commitment of American assistance to South Vietnam had
not seemed, and does not seem, on balance to
have been illegal or immoral to me. But I was
deeply impressed with the earnestness and the in-
telligence of these two human beings on the other
side. On one issue, the much-debated matter of
"reciprocity," their point of view was clear and
logical, given their premises, and worlds apart
from the official United States view of reciprocity.
The Ambassador said:

> We are not bombing your cities, your factories,
> your schools and roads and hospitals in Amer-
> ica. Once again you in America are escaping
> the horrors of war in your homeland. Our
> country has been at war for thirty years and
> you are bombing us. We cannot begin to talk
> about 'reciprocity' until you stop the bombing.
> Please—please—*please* understand our situ-
> ation as we see it.

I found myself unable to argue with his logic,
as would many who have lived on the other side,
the ravaged and brutalized other side of war
about which we know nothing.

We Americans are an underdeveloped people.
We do not know much about social revolution or
war. There is a fellowship of the bombed among
Englishmen, Germans, Russians, Chinese, Japa-
nese, Vietnamese. Both the futility and the cruelty
of some bombing policies might be more clearly
understood if London had been New York, Cov-
entry had been Cleveland, Shanghai had been

Chicago, Dresden had been Detroit, Hiroshima had been San Francisco.

On Sunday, August 6, 1967, the Eastern Europe Seminar, which it was this writer's privilege to lead, went out to Lidice. Lidice, the village that the Nazis burned in reprisal for the assassination of Reichskommandant Reinhard Heydrich. Lidice, whose men over 14 (nearly 200) were shot without exception. Lidice, a symbol of cold-blooded terror to all the world. But I kept remembering that that same day, August 6, was the 22nd anniversary of Hiroshima, when 100,-000 people were killed by a single bomb for (we said) the sake of peace. Two hundred men for terror, 100,000 for peace—how do we weigh the justice of these two acts? I was confused by the very question. The real point is that a quarter of a century later, World War II is still a dreadful living fact in Lidice and Leningrad, in Tel Aviv and Tokyo. It is not the same kind of fact for Americans, except for those of us who have lost loved ones in some distant country.

Herbert Farmer, the late British theologian whose seminar in war and peace I was privileged to attend at the Ecumenical Institute at Boston University, once told this story:

> Many years ago . . . I was preaching on the love of God; there was in the congregation an old Polish Jew who had been converted to the Christian faith. He came to me afterward and said: "You have no right to speak of the love of God until you have seen, as I have seen . . .

the blood of your dearest friends running in the gutters on a gray winter morning." I asked him how it was that, having seen such a massacre, he had come to believe in the love of God. He said that the Christian gospel first began to lay hold of him because it bade him see God—the love of God—just where he was, just where he could not but always be in his thoughts and memories—in those bloodstained streets on that gray morning. It bade him see the love of God, not somewhere else, but in the midst of just that sort of thing, in the blood and agony of Calvary. He did at least know, he said, that this was a message that grappled with the facts.[5]

And so our developing theology of peace must incorporate such facts as having enemies, brutalities, bitterness, hate—and a way of faith and life that can overcome such facts.

In the city of Berlin there stands a striking symbol of a Christian understanding of the enemy. There is a place in Bernauer Strasse where the Wall cuts through the front of a churchyard. On either side of the churchyard are bricked-up and abandoned tenements—abandoned except for the guns of the East German guards. On the West side of the Wall, memorial wreaths mark the spots where escapees from the East have been shot. The church itself is on the East side in the Soviet zone, but facing west. The building is closed. But high above the church door and the Wall itself stands a figure of the Christ, his hand upraised in benediction. Incredibly, the name of this church today is what it has been for many generations, long before the boundary was marked there or the Wall erected on its yard: The Church of the Reconciliation. And someone has painted large letters on the Wall just there: *GLAUBEN IST SEHEN,* "Seeing is believing."

This is what a theology of the enemy is all about and what this book is all about: to see the face of Christ on the other side of every dividing wall of hostility. It is to remind us that no nation, no people, no man is an absolute enemy. It is to put the church in the very midst of the greatest of human tension. It is to seek and persist in precisely the most frustrating and exasperating encounters among men, never expecting that reconciliation will be easy, or that it can be purchased without enormous patience and immeasurable sacrifice.

Chapter 2
Christoph Schmauch

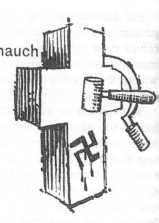

The Maze of Ideas

War is absurd. War is obsolete. Whatever may have been gained or lost in earlier wars, it is clear that everyone will lose the next war if it becomes a global military conflict. If early generations believed that war was a suitable means of settling international disputes, the advent of atomic weapons in 1945 made such a belief a fantasy. But the fantasy persists in the minds of peoples.

The causes of wars have been manifold: economic, political, social, cultural. However, underlying all these causes are ideas. They may be ideas about a nation or a race or an economic or political system or about God or religion. Frequently these ideas clash. When men are unwilling or unable to resolve the clash of ideas peacefully, they resort to force. Military power is assumed to be an instrument of justice. The victor can always claim that "might makes right."

But history will hardly support the view that greater military power is a proof of ideas. The forces most clearly embodying freedom and humanity have with terrible frequency been overwhelmed by the superior forces of death and devastation.

The burden of history shows that the church has all too often sought proof of its ideas by violence. Jesus and the early church never supported war as a viable means of settling disputes. Instead, their characteristic elements and methods of Christian discipleship were: love of enemy, reconciliation, overcoming evil with good, suffering injustice rather than inflicting it.

The Christian church, since the fourth century, has not only tolerated armed conflict, but also engaged in it as a holy obligation. It has done so on the basis of a privatized religiosity that accepts the Christian way of life as a means of dealing with the individual neighbor, but finds it impractical in international affairs. The Crusades against the "infidels" a thousand years ago and heretic hunts in the time of the Reformation and counter-Reformation, culminating in the Thirty Years War (1618-1648), are two of the most glaring examples. The struggle for political power between church and state in the Middle Ages was often violent; both were striving for absolute power and control over the known world. We must make a blunt admission of the church's failure to be the church and of the ever present possibility of its succumbing to the temptations of power. We

45

must look with an attitude of humility and repent
ance at the role of the church in the world today
As Richard Shaull puts it:

> . . . the church and its thought have been so
> identified with the old order that many modern
> revolutionaries have felt compelled to become
> atheists. The conservative position of the
> church and the irrelevance of much theology
> are so evident that nothing can be accomplished
> by attempting to cover them over; we can only
> confess what one Asian student recently de-
> scribed as the "profound humiliation" of the
> Christian in the midst of modern revolution.[1]

In order to prevent any misunderstanding
when we speak of the church being the church, we
must outline an essential element of the church's
relationship to social, political and economic structures. As a result of the struggle of the Confessing
Church with the Reich Church in Nazi Germany,
and guided by the Barmen Theses of 1934 (included in the historical confessions adopted by
the United Presbyterian Church in the U.S.A. in
1967), Christians came to realize that a reactionary mentality is the real enemy of the church. The
New Testament makes it clear beyond any doubt
that the gospel on which the church depends for
its existence is *future directed*, requiring a recep-
tivity by the church to the promise: "Behold, I
make all things new." (Rev. 21:5) It is this understanding of the mutual exclusiveness of reactionary attitudes on the one hand, and the future directed Christian existence on the other that puts

past mistakes in perspective and makes it possible today for the church to be the church. The Council of Brotherhoods of the Confessing Church declared in 1947:

> Thesis III. We have erred, when we decided to erect a Christian front against the necessary social change in the life of the people. The alliance between the Church and the powers which tried to preserve the old and the traditional has resulted in disaster. We have betrayed the Christian freedom, which permits and demands that changes in the structures of society are made, wherever such change is required for the harmonious life of the people. We have denied the right to revolution, but we have tolerated and approved the development toward an absolute dictatorship.

> Thesis V. We have erred when we overlooked the fact that the economic materialism of Marxist teaching should have reminded the Church of its task and the promise of the Christian congregation for the life of the people in community in this world. We have been amiss when we neglected to make the concern for the poor and those treated unjustly the Church's concern, according to the Gospel of the coming Kingdom of God.[2]

The church's experience with fascism could be the most painful lesson learned by the church in this century. For the danger has not passed! Its mind set is still with us. The concentration camps of Nazi Germany are only the practical application of a mentality that considers whole groups of people as inferior, and therefore subject to extermination with the most efficient means available. Let it be quite clear that anyone who seriously considers the use of atomic weapons against another nation reveals the kind of mentality that —because of the indiscriminate nature of these weapons—can only be called fascist. Vatican II, in its *Constitution on the Church in the Modern World*, put it this way: "Any act of war aimed indiscriminately at the destruction of entire cities or extensive areas along with their population is a crime against God and man himself. It merits unequivocal and unhesitating condemnation."[3]

"Dialogue Is an Objective Necessity of the Age." [4]

But what about communism? More than one hundred years ago Karl Marx, confronted with the economic, political and social situation of nineteenth century Europe, realized the need for basic structural changes in modern societies. He developed economic, political and social theories that he thought would bring about the necessary changes toward humanization of industrialized societies. Because of the reactionary nature of the Christian church in his day, atheism became a conspicuous element of Marxist ideology. Religion, according to Marx, is "the opium of the people," because it comforts those who are alienated within their society, rather than finding ways and means to eliminate the causes of this alienation, which are basically economic and

48

political. It will be useful to quote the context of the well-known phrase in order to make clear that the vulgar atheism usually associated with it is a distortion:

> Religious distress is at the same time the expression of real distress and the protest against real distress. Religion is the sigh of the oppressed creature, the heart of a heartless world, just as it is the spirit of a spiritless situation. It is the opium of the people.
>
> The abolition of religion as the illusory happiness of the people is required for their real happiness. The demand to give up the illusions about its condition is the demand to give up a condition which needs illusions. The criticism of religion is therefore in embryo the criticism of the vale of woe, the halo of which is religion.[5]

It is understandable but not excusable that the church reacted to Marxism with lack of understanding at best, with hostility and indifference at worst. We can only speculate how different world history would have been if a creative dialogue between Christians and Marxists had started one hundred years ago. However, the first attempts to implement Marxist theory were opposed not only by governments, whose power was directly challenged, but also by the churches' great interest in preserving the status quo. Stalinist brutality and the personality cult are as much a perversion of Marxism as the heresy trials and witch hunts of the Middle Ages were a terrible perversion of the nature of the Christian church. Since most Chris-

49

tians would not want the value of the Christian faith judged by the violence, brutality and inhumanity inflicted on other men in the name of Christianity, it is only fair to refrain from judging Marxism on the basis of crimes committed in its name. The gospel requires the church to oppose evil, regardless of who perpetrates it.

When we discuss the church's relationship to Marxism, we have to keep in mind that its original opposition to communism was not based on the cruelty that accompanied the implementation of Marxist theory, but rather on the atheistic element and the call for basic changes in society. In passing, we might also do well to remind ourselves that one of the most important elements of Nazi ideology was "anti-bolshevism" in the same way as "anticommunism" has characterized American thinking and foreign policy, especially since 1945. Unless we understand the church's wrong reasons for becoming the spiritual backbone of anticommunism, we cannot understand the reasons that led to the Christian-Marxist dialogue.

In 1965, President John C. Bennett of Union Theological Seminary, New York, summarized the rethinking of Christian attitudes toward communism. After dealing in detail with the changes in the communist world (characterized by the internal process of gradual individuation and humanization in communist countries), he writes:

> God does not need defense against Communist atheism. As I have said, a new generation of communists for whom atheism is an in-

herited creed has begun to ask religious questions and a new generation of Christians in both East and West is also asking questions about their inherited images of God. Official Communist atheism is a response to false stereotypes of Christianity but has no word for anyone. More serious is a self-sufficient scientism that is common to Communist and non-Communist nations alike.

The Christian Church has ahead of it a great new adventure as it faces the post-revolutionary generation in Communist countries, as Communist fanaticism dies, and as these countries slowly become open to the outside world. American Christians can have a part in these new opportunities for the Church only if they abandon their absolutistic anti-communism, if they take a positive attitude toward many of the social and economic results of Communist revolutions, and if they stand sympathetically with the people of those countries whose minds are becoming more open. There are vistas here of listening and of witnessing and of new life for us all.[6]

This summary requires further explanation. How was it possible, after one hundred years of hostility, for Christians and Marxists to enter into a creative dialogue? The revolutionary processes of this century are no longer debatable in terms of isolated interruptions of an otherwise peaceful and contented world, but are being recognized by Marxists as well as Christians as a new stage in the history of mankind. Billions of people are groping

51

for new models of organization for society, being sure of nothing else so much as the total inadequacy of present structures of particular societies and of the international community. This is most obvious in the gap between the rich and the poor, which *Newsweek* magazine discussed in "The Scandal of the Century—Rich and Poor."[7] The article points out that the developed countries must have a basic change of attitude, as well as restructuring of their economic situation in the developing world. Dr. Raul Prebisch, Secretary General of the United Nations Conference on Trade and Development, put it this way:

> I am persuaded that in the developing world a very profound economic revolution has to take place, not only an economic revolution, but a far reaching transformation of the social structure, because the developing world would be unable to assimilate modern technology at a fast enough rate without considerable and far reaching changes in the economic and social structure. This revolution is inevitable and we have to discuss what shape it must take, what degree of human sacrifice, and social and political sacrifice, of moral sacrifice, this revolution of the Third World will entail.[8]

Both Christians and Marxists must accept special responsibility in the race against disaster. "Both Marxists and Christians have one point in common, mainly a real concern for concrete man in his social environment, and both are faced with the complacency of society about man's condition."[9] In a crisis like this we need to think together about *how* we show our concern for man.

Within the Christian community, church councils and movements have begun to accept the challenge of the global situation. The Christian Peace Conference, based in Prague, described by some as a prominent participant in the left wing of the ecumenical movement, provides a good example of a dialogue that is not only a pleasant pastime for "beautiful souls," as Roger Garaudy, a leader in the dialogue from the Marxist side, has pointed out, but also a confrontation of different viewpoints through an involvement in the great events of history.[10] The nature of the involvement is always subject to reevaluation, as the participants gain new insights within the context of the ever changing historical situation. Professor Josef Hromadka, the president of the Christian Peace Conference, has made the difficult distinction between revolution and counter-revolution:

What is revolution and what is counter-revolution? Sometimes it is very difficult to make a distinction. There is the analogy in the Old Testament of the real prophets and the false prophets. Who were the real prophets? And who were the false prophets? Outwardly there was not very much difference, but there was a profound difference between Amos, Hosea, Jeremiah, and Isaiah and the many false prophets with which the Old Testament deals. In the history of our nations the problem of revolution and counter-revolution is very, very important because people are not always able to tell the difference. When the Nazi movement started in Germany many intelligent people were confused. They thought it was a real revolution, necessary revolution, and instead it proved to be a terrific, destructive counter-revolution.[11]

It should be noted that the Christian Peace Conference has its origin in the common experience of World War II and the desire of Christian leaders in Eastern and Western Europe to contribute to reconciliation between East and West. The concerns of the Christian Peace Conference have broadened over the past decade. Ten years ago the central European situation (and the German language) dominated the movement, but the Third All-Christian Peace Assembly, held in Prague March 31-April 5, 1968, made it clear that the needs and problems of "the Third World" —or, as the Asians, Africans and Latin Americans put it, "the Two-Thirds World"—must receive priority attention. Christians from the developing countries are increasingly impatient with the notion that they should be imported for decorative purposes only (as churches have often done, exploiting their colorful costumes and their colored skins to prove something or other about brotherhood): they are demanding full participation.

Christians from the Soviet Union and the socialist countries of Eastern Europe share many of the patronizing attitudes of Christians in the capitalist countries of the West. It may seem strange to Americans (and even stranger to Russians) to discover the growing tendency in the Third World to lump these two peoples together as belonging to the affluent status quo of the Northern Hemisphere. The Christian-Marxist dialogue itself is sometimes seen by Christians from the Third World as an attempt to bring about a "Pax Russo-Americana" as a common front of the developed countries against the Two-Thirds world of the developing countries. The Christian Peace Conference—and indeed the whole Christian community—is confronted with a new triangular situation in human understanding and organizational struggles.

Is it possible that Christians and Marxists in Europe and America are now able to talk to each other only because both have ceased to be authentic revolutionaries and are preoccupied with protecting their own prosperity? To the extent that this may be true, the poor nations that are still caught up in a revolutionary situation can understandably cry: "A plague on both your houses!"

A remarkable aspect of the Christian-Marxist dialogue is the growing participation of Roman Catholics. For decades, Catholic leaders sought to condemn communism and socialism in all forms and to isolate Catholics from Marxists and other revolutionaries. The Vatican dramatized its role as the defender of the faith and of established institutions against "atheistic communism."

Pope John XXIII, in his encyclical *Pacem in*

Terris ("Peace on Earth"), unleashed a modern miracle. Catholics, Protestants and followers of many religions were inspired to a new attitude of common humanity and dialogue with communists and socialists. Pope John's later encyclical *Mater et Magistra* ("Mother and Teacher"), and his successor Paul VI's encyclical *Populorum Progressio* ("On the Development of Peoples") focused Christian thought on the poverty and revolutionary social changes of the developing nations, and opened up new possibilities for Catholics in ideological discussion. Vatican II established a Department for Conversations with Non-Believers and by this act, authorized official Catholic participation in the Christian-Marxist dialogue.

These astonishing new directions in Catholic thought were echoed at the World Council Conference on Church and Society, Geneva, 1966.

> A direct dialogue is possible between Christians and advocates of non-Christian social ideologies. Specifically we urge that the World Council of Churches seek to initiate an informal dialogue with Marxists on an international basis, in each region of the world. We believe this will increase possibilities of cooperation between Christians and non-Christians, irrespective of their ideologies, for the furtherance of peace and progress for all mankind.[12]

There are indeed hopeful signs that the miracle of reconciliation between Christians and Marxists will yet come about.

Christianity and Nationalism

A nation is more than a country: it is an idea. It is an idea with a powerful grip upon men's emotions and a fateful impact upon their lives. It is not easy to take an objective, detached view of what our nation means to us. Our ultimate loyalties and our religious sentiments are very much bound up in the idea of the nation. We are startled and even offended by the wag who said: "A nation is a society united by a common error as to its origins and a common aversion to its neighbors." Yet we must understand that the idea of the nation has a history that we seldom recognize and a relationship to war and peace that is fundamental.

Nationalism is a modern movement that began in the 16th century, developed in the next two centuries and became so generally accepted as force and fact that the 19th century has been called the "age of nationalism." While the Roman Empire and the Holy Roman Empire were universal in outlook, modern nationalism emphasized the special nature of a given nationality. The Protestant Reformation resulted not only in the destruction of the monolithic power of the Roman Catholic Church, but also gave kings and princes a religious base for their struggle for greater independence from the Empire. The beginnings of modern nationalism can be understood as a protest against the heavy hand of Pope and Emperor, who failed to do justice to the ethnic, cultural and

57

historical peculiarities of the kingdoms within the Holy Roman Empire. The Puritan revolution in England in the seventeenth century may be considered a further manifestation of modern nationalism. New scientific discoveries, commercial activities and politics created an optimistic humanism that was added to the Calvinist ethic of success. There were new possibilities open to all. The English people identified themselves with ancient Israel and developed a sense of mission that spread abroad from England, a land ". . . celebrated for endless ages as a soil most genial to the growth of liberty," as John Milton says in his essay on liberty.

> Surrounded by congregated multitudes, I now imagine that I behold the nations of the earth recovering that liberty which they so long had lost; and that the people of this island are disseminating the blessings of civilization and freedom among cities, kingdoms and nations.[13]

English nationalism greatly influenced the French and American revolutions in the eighteenth century, which were based on a radical humanism. The Declaration of Independence and the famous slogan "Liberty, equality, fraternity," were expressions of this new nationalism. German romantic nationalism added an irrational element to the emerging attitudes toward the nation state. It appealed to the deepest emotions of citizens through folklore, folk songs and primitive folk traditions. Citizen armies replaced the highly trained professional armies of the eighteenth century, and embodied the old Roman faith in the sweetness of dying for the fatherland.

Napoleon's nationalism might be called "counter productive," since French occupation of European countries produced in them a strong desire for national independence. German nationalism in the nineteenth century became perverted by irrational tendencies, and eventually led to the first and second World Wars. At the end of World War I, the West began to realize that in spite of the independent destiny of nation states, actual interdependence required international cooperation. The League of Nations became the first feeble expression of this understanding, to be replaced by the United Nations in 1945. During World War II, many colonies came of age, and the postwar period saw a resurgence of nationalism as a means for gaining independence from former colonial masters. These new nations more than doubled the membership of the United Nations within twenty years. Nationalism has proved to be the most powerful force in the struggle for national liberation and independence; it has destroyed monoliths of imperialism, capitalism and communism alike.

However we evaluate the power of nationalism, we must realize that unless sovereign countries accept reasonable limitations to their national sovereignty by international law and arbitration, old wounds will never heal, and nationalist passions will continue to bring the world to the brink of disaster.

In order to illustrate the dangers of nationalism and understand the possible role of the church as an agent of reconciliation, let us look at a concrete example in recent history from the author's personal experience.

Authorities on European affairs agree that the peaceful development of the continent hinges on Germany's relationship to its neighbors. The turbulent history of 2,000 years in Central Europe furnishes the backdrop for discussion of this problem in the Federal Republic of Germany (West Germany). This discussion has been stimulated by the memorandum of 1965, of the Evangelical Church in Germany, "The Status of Expellees and the Relationship of the German People to Its Eastern Neighbors."

The Potsdam agreement of August 2, 1945, entrusted Poland with the administration of Silesia, parts of Pomerania and of East Prussia (an area bounded on the north by the Baltic Sea, on the south by Czechoslovakia, on the east by Poland and on the west by Germany: Mecklenburg, Brandenburg and Saxony). This arrangement was to last until a final settlement could be reached between the allies and Germany. The East-West conflict, and the subsequent division of Germany into occupation zones, followed by its division into the Federal Republic of Germany (West Germany) and the German Democratic Republic (East Germany) remained officially unresolved by any peace treaty, but nevertheless East Germany remains an historical fait accompli.

At the heart of the history of Silesia is the two-thousand-year-old conflict between Slavonic and Germanic groups. In the tenth century, the population of the disputed territories was exclusively Slavonic, but during the Bohemian, Hapsburg and especially during the Prussian (since 1740) periods, the German element became increasingly prominent. During the Nazi period, no German schoolbook admitted that this part of Germany had ever been anything but German.

The sad history of Nazi intolerance, power politics and racial prejudice, the systematic extermination of "inferior human beings" on the basis of a "scientific" theory of racial superiority, plus an anti-bolshevik ideology, caused the flight and expulsion of 11 million Germans from the Polish-occupied territories east of the Oder-Neisse Line. These people moved into the Federal Republic of Germany and the German Democratic Republic in the anarchy that followed Germany's unconditional surrender.

West Germany considers the matter of the Oder-Neisse Line as the permanent eastern border of Germany to be an open question. The East German Government, because of its communist affinity with Poland and its political realism, recognized the Oder-Neisse Line as its eastern border almost as soon as it was established, hailing it as a border of peace. The policy of the West German Government on the subject has been largely determined by vocal and well-organized refugee groups, which have played a considerable role in the party politics of the Federal Republic of Germany. No party could hope to win an election without the support of these people, who persistently emphasize their *Recht auf Heimat* (right to the homeland) and the restoration of Germany's borders to prewar boundaries. The situation has been further complicated by the Hallstein Doctrine, which states that no government can have diplomatic relations with the Federal Republic of Germany and at the same time recognize the German Democratic Republic as a sovereign state (nevertheless, by 1968 there were three exceptions: Romania, Yugoslavia and the Soviet Union).

It is not surprising that in an atmosphere charged with the deepest emotions on the individual and national level, encompassing the whole range of the East-West conflict, the memorandum of the Evangelical Church in Germany evoked widely varied reactions, ranging from the gratitude of those who for years had hoped for some official word that would lead out of the impasse in the discussion, to those whose mentality is best characterized by the following attack on the memorandum: "Since 1945 when the German Reich collapsed, the Evangelical Church has acted persistently in such a way as to reveal unquestionably a betrayal of state, nation and fatherland, to the advantage of Bolshevik interests. . . . It is a long way from the powerful personality of Luther, who, as a Christian and a German, attacked injustice with great courage, to today's bloodless theologian, with his foolish

62

self-accusations and confessions of guilt. The Evangelical Church in Germany is today, to the largest extent, only a burden in the struggle with Bolshevism." [14]

What then is the content of this document that calls forth such violent reactions? In the preface to the memorandum, the chairman of the Council of the Evangelical Church in Germany, Dr. Kurt Scharf, points out that after twenty years the wounds of World War II have not healed, especially those caused by the occupation of these territories by Poland and the Soviet Union. He considers it part of the church's responsibility to help men face problems, and to try to point the way to possible solutions; the church needs to act as an instrument of peace among the nations.

The guilt of the German people in relation to their neighbors is emphasized by the history of the past fifty years. There is also deep concern for the refugees and expellees, who to a large extent have achieved economic integration, but who have not yet accepted their fate and continue to insist on their *Recht auf Heimat*. On the other hand, in dealing with former German territories, the memorandum points out that Poland lost 6½ million people during World War II, which approximates 25 percent of the prewar population.

Today in Poland, communists and noncommunists, officials of the state and members of the Roman Catholic hierarchy, agree that these territories are absolutely essential to the existence of the Polish nation. Cardinal Wyszynski, Roman

Catholic Primate of Poland, has repeatedly pointed out that according to canon law, no difference exists between the authority of the bishops in the dioceses of the Western Territories and other parts of Poland.

A careful analysis of international law as it relates to Polish and German claims leads to this conclusion:

> The legal positions taken limit each other: justice confronts justice, or—more to the point —injustice stands against injustice. In such a situation the insistence on mutually contradictory legal claims becomes fruitless, even a danger to peace between the two nations. On this level, the conflict cannot be solved. Therefore an agreement has to be sought that will establish a new order between Germans and Poles. By so doing, the past is not justified, but a peaceful life together of the two peoples in the future is made possible.[15]

There are two conflicting views underlying the discussion of ethical considerations in the political realm. There are those who would emphasize the "right to the homeland" as a God-given natural right. Then there are those who emphasize the centrality of reconciliation in the political realm, and who point out that "right" is not so much a metaphysical theory as a dynamic possibility in the context of Christian forgiveness. The authors of the memorandum agree that the mutual acceptance of guilt is a prerequisite for reconciliation and a new beginning.

It is evident from this example that the message of reconciliation presents the last recourse in the solution of international problems when there is no clear-cut legal solution. And it can be said of most conflicts that justice confronts justice or injustice stands against injustice.

Ecumenical Frontiers and the Quest for Peace

Religion may help to solve some human problems, but religion itself is one of the biggest problems of all. Religious ideas not only deal with the problem of international conflict, they are also part of the problem itself. The bearers of the message of reconciliation also bear the marks of conflict within and among religious groups. Religion may promote peace, but it may also prove to be the chief obstacle to peace.

The interrelationship between the ecumenical movement and the quest for peace should be self-evident. Preaching what we do not practice is an offense and a scandal. We should not be surprised that a credibility gap exists between the so-called Christian nations of the white, Northern hemisphere and the rest of the world. It will not be easy to undo the damage.

Communication and travel have made it possible for Christians from all parts of the world to meet and consult with one another on international affairs. In a chapter entitled "To the Ends of the Earth," Colin Williams summarizes:

"International Affairs" is the area where perhaps the least progress has been made towards breaking down the walls of separation, fear, and suspicion; and it is the area where dangers to human community have reached their height. In the matter of the ancient enmity between racial groups the churches are showing signs of breaking free from their imprisonment in the ways of the world. But in this arena of international relations there are as yet no comparable signs.[16]

Nothing less than an international church strategy will have to be developed to make the best use of present structures, and to devise new instruments for carrying out a reconciling and prophetic ministry on a global scale. The World Council of Churches, the Vatican and regional organizations in Asia, Africa, America and Europe are trying to develop such a strategy. But much needs to be done in the whole area of education. Recent sociological studies have confirmed for the membership of the churches what Gunnar Myrdal pointed out for the general population: "In none of the existing national cultures are people educated to know and like people in other countries who are different from themselves; on the contrary, they are often indoctrinated with national self-righteousness and are apt to despise, fear and hate those who are outside the nation and live differently."

The goal must be the education of a *new international man*, who is able to put himself in the other person's place, and who is equipped to try to understand the different values that motivate

THE MAZE OF IDEAS

individuals and nations. This requires a high level of security and a low level of defensiveness, a part of what the New Testament calls "Christian maturity." If a certain degree of this maturity exists, it will be easier to perceive the reality of the world in which we live, to interpret historical events and to analyze the international situation accurately. Most people have opinions and judgments about major events, but because of faulty data and fallacious theories they arrive at wrong conclusions. They say: "I have my own ideas. Don't confuse me with facts—or with anybody else's ideas!"

We are fortunate that in the church today the data for intelligent judgment can be supplied from many sources through the communications media. The exchange of information enables us better to understand ourselves and people from other parts of the world, who perceive developments from a different point of view and describe them in the context of their own background and experience.

The war in Vietnam has found the churches wanting, not only in understanding of the history of that tortured country, but also in knowledge of the religion of the majority of the Vietnamese people: Buddhism. The overriding reason for this ignorance is a missionary attitude that did not try to understand in order to appreciate but only to destroy Buddhist beliefs in order to make converts. A number of other reasons are mentioned in a statement made by the Protestant-Orthodox-Catholic Consultation on Dialogue with Men of Other Faiths, in Kandy, Ceylon in 1967:

A tragedy of our worldwide situation today, however, is that, generally speaking, Christians are satisfied with coexistence, instead of entering into that continuous and growing dialogical relationship in which the whole of life becomes life with and for others. Hesitations and difficulties are, of course, felt on both sides. Christians, who have to repent of and live down much sad history, have thereby a special responsibility for building bridges of understanding. They have to challenge in themselves unexamined assumptions of superiority, and remove many inhibitions, arising from fear and suspicion of the unknown, lack of real confidence in the Living Lord, and uncertainty as to the attitude they ought to adopt to a different religious tradition. There is far too much Christian communalism and ghettoism—in both West and East.[17]

Christians in the United States have had to learn the hard way about Roman Catholic involvement in Vietnam, and the less than glorious history of mission activity in that country. In his foreword to *Vietnam: Lotus in a Sea of Fire* by the Buddhist monk, Thich Nhat Hanh, Thomas Merton, a Roman Catholic monk, writes:

Certainly these pages make a Catholic squirm with embarrassment. They should do so. The Second Vatican Council has clearly admitted that there is no place left for empty triumphalism in the Catholic estimate of missionary history. Serious errors have been made, and they have brought great discredit on the Christian message. These errors were due not to the faith and to the Gospel, but to nationalistic and cultural prejudices, attachment to rigid organizational patterns, or obsession with institutional façades and political prestige. The Council has implicitly or explicitly admitted such errors, and has declared that they must never be repeated.[18]

If we really want to understand, we have to listen to the other side, even if it is painful. This is the way a Buddhist monk sees it:

The attitude of the early missionaries toward the traditional native culture and religion and the language used to express that attitude caused much strife and destruction. Later this situation was worsened when a number of Catholics showed their dependence on and alliance with the colonial government and then the Ngo Dinh Diem regime. The influence of the Catholic clergy, in particular the French priests, was all too obvious under the French Occupation and even throughout the Indochina war (1946-1954). Anyone in trouble, particularly political trouble, could find a safe haven if he asked for the local priest's intervention. Arrests and threats were commonplace under French rule, especially after the return of French troops to Indochina. Under these conditions, the protection and guarantee of safety by the priest was a great source of security. Many people converted to Roman Catholicism out of gratitude for the father's service of this nature. But many had to convert because they had no other choice.[19]

How different might history have been if Roman Catholics and Buddhists had treated one another with mutual respect rather than with hostility, and how much suffering could have been prevented if a Christian-Buddhist dialogue had taken place in Vietnam in past decades!

What we have said so far makes it clear that the quest for peace makes dialogue with people of all ideologies and religions absolutely necessary. The Israeli-Arab conflict, which exploded into war in 1967, has crucial religious implications. Men on both sides will freely admit the mystique that is so much a part of the struggle for the control of "holy places." During this conflict, Christians and Jews in the United States were shocked when they discovered that in spite of their interfaith encounter in the civil rights movement and in the peace movement, they did not understand each other on the level of their deepest emotions. Most Jews took Christian support for the cause of Israel for granted, and were greatly disappointed when this support was not forthcoming without reservations. Some Christian leaders did point out the other side of the story, especially having in mind the Arab refugees and the religious basis of the state of Israel, which, by its very nature, tends to be discriminatory toward other religious backgrounds, and unwilling to accept the pluralism of a modern, democratic and open society.

This crisis in Christian-Jewish relations made it perfectly clear that a much greater depth in dialogue will be required if "the truth in love" is to be spoken and heard even when one of the partners in the dialogue finds it nearly impossible to be objective because his special interests are at stake.

If we are not to make the same mistakes over and over again, mistakes that we no longer can afford to make, we will have to learn to anticipate rather than merely to react to emergencies in international affairs. Because of the complexity of today's conflicts, we have to know and understand as much as is humanly possible in order to make intelligent judgments to bring about the necessary reconciliation between ideas and forces, *before* these crises erupt in violence and human slaughter.

Chapter 3
Daisuke Kitagawa

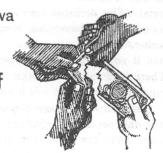

The Maze of Race and Economics

At the turn of the century, W. E. B. Du Bois boldly stated that "The problem of the twentieth century is the problem of the color line—the relation of the darker to the lighter races of men in Asia and Africa, in America and the islands of the sea." [1] Events since World War II have more than borne out the truth of his prediction. Thoughtful people today are seriously concerned whether the racial conflict so prevalent throughout the world may inevitably lead mankind into World War III. They wonder if all the serious economic, social and political conflicts may after all be basically racial in character. [2]

New Militancy on the Part of the Colored Races

No one can fail to see how militant the peoples whose skins have colored pigmentation have become in recent years. They appear to be growing increasingly so. The Black Muslim movement in the United States is a forerunner of this trend.[3] The American public is being confronted by the challenge of Black Power advocates. Many white Americans are saying, "Negroes have never had it so good. Why are they so discontented?" There is obviously something distorted about this point of view.

Until a few years ago, the civil rights movement was the concerted efforts of enlightened black, white and other Americans to achieve racial integration at all levels and in all sectors of American life. This goal has not been completely accomplished. The more articulate black people today sound as if they are striving for an independent development of black people separate from white people.[4]

Some of the radical leaders in the Black Power movement seem to be saying that the old civil rights leaders' approach is no longer tenable. They consider people like Roy Wilkins of the National Association for the Advancement of Colored People (NAACP), Whitney Young of the National Urban League, the late Dr. Martin Luther King, Jr., of the Southern Christian Leadership Conference (SCLC), and a host of other distinguished black Americans to be little less than "white men's Negroes." Moreover, they give the impression that they mean what they seem to be saying by pointing to the recent race riots. They declare that a riot immediately accomplishes more than all the civil rights laws put together, even at great cost in human life and property. One thing is clear: black people are not content to be merely accepted by the white man into the white man's society on the white man's terms. The black American is determined to assert himself as an American in his own right and on his own terms.

The Black Muslim and the Black Power movements in America are both antedated by similar movements in Africa, beginning with the Pan-Africanism championed by George Padmore;[5] the doctrine of Negritude in French-speaking Africa, of which Aimé Césaire and Léopold Sédar Senghor are noted advocates;[6] the emphasis on "African Personality" in English-speaking Africa; and the striving to establish "black governments" in the wake of decolonization all over Africa. Undergirding all these movements are the Western-educated African intellectuals, who for the past few decades have been preoccupied with the effort to restore African identity to their cultural life.[7]

The Communist Revolution in China in 1948, and the subsequent isolation of the People's Republic from the Western world have helped China assert her national identity as distinct from that of the white man. There are other strong racial overtones in that China is eager to establish close relationships with all the developing Afro-Asian nations, offering them all sorts of technical aid while keeping her door adamantly closed to both the USSR and the West.[8]

One World Indivisible: The Context of Interracial Encounter

One of the striking facts of life in the second half of the twentieth century is that the technologically advanced and economically affluent West is being confronted by the increasingly militant Afro-Asian and Latin American nations. This confrontation is taking place as a direct and inevitable consequence of the colonial expansion of the West during the preceding three centuries. It was discussed extensively at the World Conference on Church and Society in Geneva in 1966.

At that conference, professionally competent participants from many parts of Africa, Asia and Latin America articulated both their aspirations and their frustrations. Christians and non-Christians alike expressed their common desire for their nations to be independent, to assert their respective national identities and to be responsible partners with their former colonial masters in the common task of building the new world community. They expressed their frustration for not being able to achieve this dream because of the growing economic gap between their countries and the North Atlantic countries.

In this encounter three things became clear. 1) The encounter was, among other things, between the rich and the poor countries. The vast majority of the rich countries were more or less north of the 38th parallel, and practically all the poor countries south of it. This is the frequently referred to "North and South conflict." [9] 2) The same encounter was almost ipso facto between the white race and the colored races. This implies that the economically affluent, technologically advanced countries are largely inhabited by people of the Caucasian race, while the poor and developing countries are inhabited largely by those of Negro, Mongolian and other so-called colored races.[10] 3) Almost all the countries in the latter category were colonies of those in the former category.

The confrontation between two groups of nations at the present moment of human history cannot be anything but painful. We may even wish that such a confrontation between "have" and "have-not" nations, between established and developing nations, between the white and the colored races could be avoided. But the confrontation between the two sectors of the world is inevitable. Today the only remaining question to be answered is whether the confrontation will lead to the explosion of the whole world, or whether it will result in a mutual reconciliation in a global community.

But why is the confrontation inevitable? The answer is simple: because the two sectors are already integral parts of a world society, interdependent upon each other. This has occurred as a logical consequence of Western colonial imperialism. Through Western colonial imperialism, technological civilization has embraced all of mankind in one economic unit. The world has been compressed into a single entity, and ". . . as a result, what was once a gulf which divided two wholly separate worlds is rapidly becoming a rift which divides one self-conscious human community." [11]

In 1917, President Wilson proclaimed that ". . . there must not be a balance of power, but a community of power, not organized rivalries, but an organized common peace." Commenting on this statement, the British historian, Professor Geoffrey Barraclough, says:

> . . . in spite of their rivalry, Wilson and Lenin had one thing in common: their rejection of the existing international system. . . . They were the "champion revolutionists of the age," "the prophets of a new international order." [12]

From Racial Stratification to Racial Polarization

The rich and poor nations, developing nations and their former colonial masters have been brought to confrontation with each other in a context of a potential world society. It is here that racial tensions between the have and have-not nations come to a head to determine the course of events for the immediate future. As Ronald Segal has said,

> It is the correspondence of rich with white and poor with colored across so much of mankind that promises, by adding to the insurrection of poverty the passion of race, such a future (i.e., race war). The economic may well be the dominant cause; but the racial may be-

come the dominant identification. What has begun as economic discontent has frequently ended in nationalist upheaval. And is the racialist affiliation inherently less powerful than the nationalist one? The Chinese are not alone in increasingly seeing the economic struggle through tinted lenses.[13]

It used to be a common practice among people of goodwill to reduce the race problem to either a matter of education or economics. It was almost as if by becoming more informed or by somehow being assured of economic security, people of all races would automatically get over group prejudice and group antagonism with the result that all forms of racial discrimination would suddenly disappear. Now the problem has begun to seem simpler, and at the same time more complex: no matter what the basic cause or proposed solution may be, the problem seems to be racial.

There is obviously grave danger in this situation. To complicate matters, it seems as if man has regressed rather than progressed in the area of race relations. There are many white people in the United States who are convinced that the 1954 decision to end school segregation and the Civil Rights Act of 1964 have seriously set back racial harmony in this country. However, it is not true that racial awareness is necessarily bad. I for one do not believe it is necessarily bad. In fact, I believe it is—whether good or bad—an absolutely necessary and inescapable stage that mankind must work through before authentic reconciliation can take place between the races. There is a sense in which Black Power is an indispensable element for the "redemption of American life" and for the healing of the nations.[14]

However, this does not in any way imply that there is no danger in the mounting tide of racial consciousness and sensitivity on the part of the oppressed, dispossessed people at home and abroad. I am painfully aware of the time bomb contained in the racism that is prevalent among the rising new generations. At the same time, I am not entirely blind to the tremendously creative possibilities inherent in it. There is a Chinese phrase for crisis that is made up of two characters indicating "danger" and "opportunity" respectively. As in the Chinese, crisis is a dangerous opportunity, and we can see both the danger and the opportunity in the newly aroused racial pride throughout the world.

Three points need to be stressed at this juncture: 1) the sociology of the context in which the recently decolonized peoples confront their former masters; 2) the history of their relationship with each other during the colonial period; 3) the biography of people involved in the encounter.

The context is the emerging one-world society, a society that is a good place to be for the advanced, white nations. But for the developing nations of predominantly colored races, it is a miserable place, in some ways even more miserable than before they gained their independence. In the past, they either were resigned to their state of misery, or else they did not know better. But now they know that it is not necessary for them to stay poor, and they are daily exposed to the luxurious life that is led in the other half of the world that is enjoying an unprecedented state of affluence. This means, among other things, that the colored races are committed to radical change of the status quo, while the white race is more inclined to try to keep the status quo.

The affluent white race is thus basically peace oriented, while the colored races, in the wake of their decolonization, are basically justice oriented. Within this context, the peace that the white man seeks seems to the others to be nothing but the perpetuation of the injustices imposed upon them by the social, economic and political structures of a white dominated world. On the other hand, the desire for justice by the nonwhite world is seen by the white race as nothing short of a socio-economic revolution. The conflict of interest is thus inevitable.

At this point the history of the relationship between the two further complicates the situation. From one point of view it is a history of the conquest and enslavement of the colored races by the white race. From the opposite point of view, it is a history of the gradual emancipation of the colored races from the tyranny of the raw forces of untamed nature, the transition from pre-industrial to industrial economy and the growing dependence of the white race on the colored races to provide raw materials and cheap labor.

80

The period since Vasco da Gama up to World War II is thus to the white race a period of maritime imperialism and industrial and economic expansion at the expense of the colored races. To the colored races, it is a shameful period of colonization and enslavement, filled with painful memories. But the fact remains that it is this period in which the foundation of the one-world society was laid down, and in which mutual interdependence between white and colored races began to be established. Thus it is not surprising that the white race tends to glory in the past and dread the future, while the colored races are more inclined to forget the past and glory in the future.

This history has been internalized in contemporary man's personal life, his biography. A white man confronting a man of a colored race embodies in himself that history in which his own race dominated the world of the colored races. And quite innocently, without thinking and without meaning to, he faces every man of colored skin with an attitude of superiority, not so much with animosity or despising, let alone hatred, as with a vague sense of being superior. By the same token, a man of the colored races confronting a white man automatically feels the burden of history deep down in himself and finds himself fighting against the inferiority complex that has become a part of his "cultural heritage."

This is why it is almost impossible for even the most liberal of white liberals to be completely free from some vestige of paternalism toward people

81

of the colored races, and even for the most highly cultured man of a colored race not to be somehow belligerent toward people whom he identifies as white. In short, there can hardly be a natural or authentic man-to-man encounter, unhampered by the history of Western colonial imperialism of the last four centuries, between a white man and a man of a colored race—at least for the foreseeable future. Man cannot be raceless, nor can human relationships be without the racial dimension for a long time to come. Man cannot divorce himself from his history. The twentieth-century man will remain a racial man, regardless of which race or races he may belong to, besides being an economic man, organization man and man of culture.

Irrepressible Claim to Peoplehood

The issue at stake is not constituted by physiological and cultural differences, but rather by the distortions of man's outlook and thought patterns. He is a product of the collective experience of his racial group, especially if he comes from a racially stratified or polarized society. One can hardly help "thinking white" or "thinking black" in contemporary United States society, where white and black are sharply polarized one against the other.

If we take colonial Africa as an example, we see that the ruling white always "thought white," never questioning its rightness or soundness, let alone validity. This attitude led him to create a certain set of educational and cultural criteria for black people as a minimum standard for them to become at all acceptable as his social equals. Those black people who made the grade (called *assimilados* in Portuguese territories or *évolués* in French areas) were treated as if they had been transformed into Portuguese or Frenchmen or Belgians, their black skin notwithstanding. In the British territories, neither technical education nor cultural adaptation nor the combination of the two was sufficient to transform a black man into an Englishman. He became at best a black Englishman, that is to say, his black skin stood in the way of complete acceptance into the colonial society. However, it was assumed that he would lead his own people when and if they were believed by the British to be ready for independence.

What is of crucial importance here is that in each case the standards for acceptance were set up unilaterally by white colonials strictly on their own terms. Black people were forced to "think white" in order to be acceptable to the white man. Those who could not do so were labeled as uncivilized, and those who refused to do so were branded as rebels. Exactly the same state of affairs has prevailed in the United States in the realm of black-white relationships. White America, always "thinking white," has not fully accepted black people who do not think as they do, and until recently black Americans have been forced to accommodate themselves to white men's criteria. For a Negro physically to pass as white has been taboo in white society, but for him to insist on "thinking black" has made him suspect in white America. This double standard has made life in America for Negro Americans no less a colonial situation than that of indigenous people of any colony in Africa or Asia.[15] But there has been a difference in America: in the white society the black man was neither to assimilate nor to stand on his own feet, but rather to remain subservient to the white man. In short, as leaders such as Stokeley Carmichael have put it, the Negro has long been denied his "peoplehood." [16]

Black Power in America, Negritude in former French Africa, African Personality in former British Africa are all expressions of the black man's aspiration to claim his peoplehood, without which he is destined to remain insecure in the white-dominated world. Within America, Black Power is not alone in what it is trying to achieve. It identifies itself with Black Nationalism in various parts of Africa. It is reflected in Red Power, the movement of university educated American Indians to reassert within the constitutional framework of the United States their lost sense of peoplehood.[17] It is reflected, too, in the trend among black students at the nation's major universities to form a variety of Afro-American student associations.

These movements cannot be dismissed as a stage or a phase that we must pass through before a fully matured and integrated America emerges, nor can they be dismissed as a current reaction to the civil rights emphasis on integration. They

must be accepted as one of the important precon-
ditions for true, authentic reconciliation among
racial communities, given the historical context.[18]

Implications for Christian Mission and Ministry

The habitat of man in the second half of the
twentieth century is one world indivisible, yet
having an economic rift running between the industrialized white north and the preindustrial-
ized colored south. Less than one-third of the
world's population and almost four-fifths of the
world's wealth are to be found in the former, and
more than two-thirds of the population and barely
one-fifth of the wealth in the latter.[19]

> Average per capita income is more than ten
> times as great in the more advanced nations as
> a whole than in the less advanced nations taken
> together, and discrepancies run higher than fifty
> to one between the richest nation, the United
> States, and the poorest ones. Worst of all, the
> contrast between rich and poor is growing
> greater, since the rich nations are moving ahead
> proportionally more rapidly than the poor coun-
> tries.[20]

To intensify the tensions between the two in-
extricably interdependent halves of the world, the
rich north (including the Soviet bloc) is Christian
in religious heritage as well as Caucasian in race,
while the poor south is anything but Christian in
religious heritage. This religious-racial-economic
gap between the two sectors of "a now unitary
world," to borrow Dr. Reischauer's phrase, not

85

only makes these tensions explosive but also makes the Christian's task extremely difficult.

The Christian church at its most ecumenical level is truly worldwide. Beginning with the Reformation and the Counter-Reformation, the church has included all races and nationalities within its community. But it is also true that Christianity is so identified with the Western powers that many non-Christians, especially in Asia and Africa, regard the church as a tool of Western imperialism.

Christians in the West all too often find themselves under the spell of what might be called a majority psychology or a superiority complex in their attitude toward the three-fourths of the world's population that is neither Christian nor caucasian. This attitude has developed because the Christian missionary movement originated for the most part in the older part of Christendom (which coincides with the rich northern half of the world) and moved to the major portion of what now constitutes the poor southern half of the world. The missionaries traveled southward with the attitude of bringing truth to the ignorant heathen. They were superior to the rest of the world in natural science, technology, engineering, industry and economics, and they fell into the trap of thinking that those who were neither Christian nor caucasian were by nature inferior. This way of thinking led the Christian missionary movement to be philanthropically oriented in its foundations.

Many Christians believed that the Caucasian West had attained its highly developed state of civilization because it had been Christian for centuries; thus the evangelistic attitude, though basically philanthropic, was in practice translated into a civilizing mission by exterminating all forms of paganism. The inevitable result was that Christian missions in Asia and Africa were dominated by what can be called the "conquest motif" in regard to all other religions.

The so-called civilizing process meant in effect that Asians and Africans had to be culturally denationalized and religiously Westernized if they were to meet the standards of civilization imposed on them by the Christian missionaries. Their peoplehood was not respected, and converts to Christianity had to be uprooted from the soil of their indigenous culture as a prerequisite or a consequence of conversion. Thus the "new" man that the missionaries produced was something less than man in that he had been completely cut off from his own people. To make matters worse, he was never fully accepted into any Western colonial community, Christian or otherwise, within his own country. He was turned into a stranger in his own land among his own people.

Although this is past history, it is recent enough to be vividly remembered by all the peoples in the poor half of the world. They are preoccupied with the task of restoring their peoplehood and establishing economic, social and political independence. Christians cannot but be suspect in their eyes. How, then, can the church carry out its mission? Or more fundamental yet, what is the mission of the church to the poor half of the world that is non-Christian and noncaucasian? We are not talking here of the mission of the churches in the West to the rest of the world, but rather of the ecumenical church throughout the world that embraces Christians of all nations, regardless of their economic or political status.

The mission of the ecumenical community in the emerging world society is not so much to christianize non-Christians as to humanize all forms of human relationships. In the area of race relations, this means that the church strives not for the assimilation (or integration) of members of minority races into a society ruled by a dominant race, but rather for the establishment of the peoplehood of all racial and ethnic groups in order to bring about a truly pluralistic society.

This means that the mission of the church within the context of a still racially stratified and polarized world is not so much to strive for peace as for justice. A peace that is not built on the foundation of justice cannot be either a just peace or a durable peace. Justice, too, needs to be translated into concrete economic, technological, political and social terms. It needs to be expressed in collective and structural terms, rather than personal and individual terms. For example, in the area of race relations, it is not enough for individual Christians to become personally free from prejudice. The church needs to help to mobilize and consolidate all the forces of justice in order to bring about a structural change in society so that the peoplehood of every racial and ethnic group can be asserted in mutual respect and trust one for another.

For the church to be able to fulfill such a mission it needs to impress upon its members, especially those in the richer areas of the world, the need to be emancipated from every shred of the majority psychology (which is the same as Professor Johannes Hoekenidjk's so-called "crusader syndrome"). Christians must outgrow their naïve faith that Christianity has the final answer to every kind of human problem, and that the role of a Christian in any situation is that of the giver, the teacher, the helper—in short, the philanthropist.

This means, among other things, that the philanthropic orientation of Christian mission is totally inadequate in the face of the growing economic gap between the two halves of the world. Millions of CARE packages will not bring about a world in which the living standard of three-fourths of its population is elevated as much as one percent. Even the massive economic and technical foreign aid programs of advanced nations are far from adequate. Dr. Raul Prebisch, General Secretary of the United Nations Conference on Trade and Development, stated at the World Council of Churches' World Conference on Church and Society, Geneva, 1966:

> In 1961 the proportion of resources transferred to developing countries was approaching

the target of one percent envisioned by the Development Decade of the United Nations, that is to say 0.87 percent. . . . But that is not all. World Bank leaders have expressed their great concern about the fact that 50 percent of the new resources transferred from industrial countries to developing countries was absorbed and cancelled out by payments for financial services received from the developed countries. This 50 percent is an average. In some countries and in some groups of countries—for instance in the Latin American region—another study has shown that in recent years the payments for financial and debt services from Latin America to the industrial centers of the world have cancelled out the resources transferred to them. And sometimes payments even exceeded the amount of the new resources. . . .[21]

What does this say to us? For one thing, it says that the developed countries' obligation toward the developing countries cannot begin to be discharged by foreign aid programs, however massive and efficient they may be. I say "obligation" because the West owes its affluence to the Third World. As Franz Fanon has put it:

This European opulence is literally scandalous, for it has been founded on slavery, it has been nourished with the blood of slaves and it comes directly from the soil and from the subsoil of that underdeveloped world. The wellbeing and the progress of Europe have been built up with the sweat and the dead bodies of Negroes, Arabs, Indians and the yellow races.[22]

The basic issue confronting today's world is that ex-colonies have been left virtually without capital and without technical skills necessary to be producers in the world industrial economy. Besides being merely providers of raw material and cheap labor, they are forced to be consumers of goods manufactured overseas. They belong to the same economic orbit as their former colonial masters, but they find the very structure of international trade against them. For being "sellers of raw commodities—too often of only one commodity per country . . . they are dependent for their foreign earnings on goods whose prices are notoriously unstable." [23]

> The price of copper, for instance, rose by 42 percent from 1954 to 1955, then plunged by 34 percent in 1957 and by as much again in 1958. Coffee rose by 38 percent from 1953 to 1954, fell by 27 percent the next year and by 33 percent in 1958. Wool fell by over 50 percent from 1952 to 1958; cocoa by as much in the single year 1956. Such fluctuations can deal staggering blows. It has been estimated, for instance, that for every penny by which copper falls on the New York market, the Chilean treasury loses four million dollars, and that each penny drop in the price of green coffee costs Latin America fifty million dollars. [23]

How can the developing countries build up the capital, structures and skilled human resources they so desperately need? Nothing short of a radical reformulation of the basic structure of international trade will be equal to this problem. This is the center of the Christian mission of this generation. It requires that Christians of all walks of life throughout the world become active, intelligent and responsible participants in corporate action in the social, economic and political arenas. For American Christians, this means putting pressure on their government to change its international trade policy. It is only by collective action that an international situation will come into being that will be more conducive to the ministry of reconciliation between the rich and poor nations and between the white and colored races.

Reconciliation cannot take place unless the parties involved are autonomous entities, each standing on its own ready to forgive and be forgiven, to give and receive. Reconciliation of black people with white people and white people with black people is not the same as integration of black people into the white man's society or the white man's concession to the black man's demands. Reconciliation between black and white cannot be realized until the peoplehood of both is asserted with self-respect by one and accepted with respect by the other, from black to white and from white to black.

Epilogue

Many white Christians of affluent America may find the significance of this difficult to understand. To them the statement of the late Rabbi Morris Adler may prove helpful:

Being at ease is a luxury reserved for majorities. They are at home in a world which is their world. The society about them reflects their image and its culture is their culture. Their superior numbers provide them with a massive stability and also, paradoxically, permit them to relax in a restful anonymity. Blending with their environment, they are not conspicuous or visible in their racial, religious, or cultural aspect. No outer force, no inner memory impels them to ask: "Who am I?"

But a minority is a breach in the wall of homogeneity, an "outsider," a deviant. The Western World is Christian, the Jew is not. Now he may not be a fervent follower of his tradition; he may even doubt its value or validity. But his birth has stamped him a Jew. Indeed he may become Unitarian or Protestant or Catholic and renounce his faith but, alas, he retains a sense of difference, for he is not native to his new creed. Overt and palpable exclusions strengthen his sense of difference; so do the subtle diminutions of full acceptance he is bound to encounter. Hence he is driven to ask: "What is this thing called Jewishness which makes the difference?[24]

Replace "Jew" and "Jewishness" with Negro and Negro-ness, African and African-ness, Asian and Asian-ness—whatever the race, Rabbi Adler's statement is applicable to all people whose peoplehood has somehow been impaired if not completely destroyed by those whom they believe constitute the dominant group.

Chapter 4
Gerard N.T. Widdrington

The Maze of International Organization

Nearly fifty years ago, many people of good conscience heaved a collective sigh of relief and assigned all the nasty, complicated problems of getting the nations and peoples of the world to live together to a magnificent creation they called the League of Nations. It failed. The pomposity of its opening words betrayed it: "We, the High Contracting Parties. . . ." It was an agreement by sovereign governments to maintain under a set of rules the political predominance given them by World War I.

At that moment in history it seemed that peace could be preserved by the maintenance of a happy status quo among the victors; there was little searching for the economic roots of discontent or the ethical bases of colonial rights. This does not mean that Wilson's fourteen points had no validity; they were the voice of conscience that caught the imagination and enthusiasm of those whose inner attitudes motivated their desire for peace. In rejecting the League, the United States Senate preferred a hardheaded distrust of the European *corps diplomatique* to the role of crusading leadership in a world of cynics. The point is: what difference is there between the United Nations today and the League 30 years ago? Who rides high today: man the political animal, man the military animal, man the economic animal, man the social animal, man the moral animal?

The charter of the United Nations that emerged at the San Francisco conference toward the close of World War II was influenced by knowledge of the mass destruction of human life in noncombatant areas, the ghastly story of the concentration camps, the de-escalation of human values (even though the final horror of the Bomb had not yet appeared)—all these conditions of war had their effect. This context is reflected in the preamble of the charter: "We the peoples. . . ." The preamble is clear proof of changed concepts of international cooperation. Although military men were in the driver's seat at the convention, the power of social, economic and moral forces in the world could not be ignored. Thus a document emerged that struck first at the roots of colonialism, even though its provisions for nonautonomous territories seemed weak. It established a trusteeship system that had teeth and held the line against any new land grabbing in the name of international authority.

95

The charter also created a major organ to deal with economic and social problems, and gave it power not only to coordinate the efforts of the Specialized Governmental Agencies, but also to enlist the cooperation of private nongovernmental organizations. In addition, it suggested the reinforcement of the Economic and Social Council by regional associations to carry out its purposes to meet the special economic needs of its continental divisions. Finally, it gave the council power to conduct specific operations, as distinct from planning and research, in these fields.

But the most important aspect of the economic and social portion of the charter is its spelling out of the need for the peoples to concern themselves with basic human rights. The emphasis on human rights appears in the preamble, "To reaffirm faith in fundamental human rights, in the dignity and worth of the human person, in the equal rights of men and women of nations large and small. . . ." and throughout the charter: ". . . in promoting and encouraging respect for human rights and for fundamental freedoms for all without distinction as to race, sex, language or religion. . . ." (Article 1, 3); ". . . assisting in the realization of human rights and fundamental freedoms. . . ." (Article 13, 1b); ". . . universal respect for and observance of, human rights. . . ." (Article 55, c); ". . . It may make recommendations for the purpose of promoting respect for and observance of human rights and fundamental freedoms for all." (Article 62, 2);

". . . The Economic and Social Council shall set up commissions in the economic and social fields and for the promotion of human rights. . . ." (Article 68). (The Commission on Human Rights is the only commission that the charter specifically creates.)

The charter implies that individuals can still be heard above the clash of powers, the high-pitched emotionalism of debate, the distortions of propaganda and the greed that seeks to retain or acquire a greater share of the world's riches. This is not to say that the actual politics involved in development and procedures in the field of human rights have been free of any of these faults. The recent debate on religious tolerance produced a fiery and highly intolerant argument, including a famous incident on a stormy day in the Trusteeship Council chamber, when an unusually angry Soviet representative was goaded into denouncing the Christian God as a "stooge" of Western imperialism, to be greeted as he concluded by a vivid flash of lightning and a crash of thunder. This caused one representative to remark, "God is exercising his right of reply!"

The whole process of hammering broad principles of human rights into concise forms is long and wearisome. Never have so many people with beams in their own eyes discerned motes in the eyes of their critics and vice versa. The second stage of implementing and enforcing the agreements is even more difficult than the formative process. It comes up hard against an essential contradiction in the charter: human rights know no national boundaries. How, then, can the interdiction of Article 2, 7 of the charter, which states that the United Nations is not "to intervene in matters which are essentially within the domestic jurisdiction of any state," be overcome? The intention in the charter's preamble ". . . to practice tolerance and live together in peace with one another as good neighbors," involves strange processes: the Soviet citizen empathizes with the distressed American Negro; the Western writer reaches out to his censored brother in East Germany; the Muslim denounces the fate of his Kashmiri or Jordanian brother; the cries of illiterate, undernourished children, marketless farmers and oppressed minorities are all heard in the relentless give and take of United Nations debate.

The structure of the United Nations is and must be based on a fundamental political agreement. Without it there can be no restraining influence over the use of force, no focus for the exercise of diplomacy. But since the area of political consensus is a limited one, it follows that the authority of the United Nations must also be minimal. Hence we have the abundance of peacekeeping expediencies, combined with an almost total lack of peacemaking achievements. Armistice and cease-fire lines still cross Kashmir, Palestine, Korea and Cyprus; there is little or no shooting, but there is also no peace, no healing, no reconciliation.

The fault lies not in the organization as an institution per se; the fault lies in the condition of political morality that envelops almost all its member states. For example, every one of the so-called great powers has been caught in bare-faced lying. Adlai Stevenson (almost certainly with complete ignorance) in the Bay of Pigs crisis, Britain and France in the Suez crisis, Valerian Zorin of Russia in the Cuban missile crisis. False witness in one form or another is part and parcel of the diplomatic picture. What of the myth (or is it one?) that no Arab political leader could avoid assassination more than a few days if he ". . . betrayed his country into peace with Israel." How, then, can peace be made when Israel has a companion myth that no Israeli politician could afford to give back her prewar conquests to the Arabs?

Pious cries for peace in this and other confrontations appear before the United Nations muffled and cloaked in impossible conditions. Obviously the justification for the United Nations cannot lie in the exemplary behavior of its members, nor in the model it provides for reasoned and honest negotiation. Rather, it lies in its ability to muster enough diplomatic skill and use of official and unofficial intercommunication to produce ingenious expediencies. If this were not so, the United Nations would have long since disintegrated. A hard-nosed nation like Russia would not have held to it for more than twenty years if it did not make sound political sense to do so, especially in view of the constant snubs and rebuffs that Russia received in the early years of the United Nations.

Each power can use the United Nations both as a brake and as a pedal: a brake on the rising power of a Secretary General by the threat of a troika, or a pedal by embarrassing its opponents in the course of developments in a situation like that in Rhodesia, the Dominican Republic or Djibouti. Finally there is recourse to the veto. The same skills and alternatives are open to all the great powers except one: the one great power who is still not a member is Communist China.

China is not a member of the United Nations not only because of the skill of United States diplomacy, but also because China's policy is geared only to China's control over any given situation. Indonesia's departure from the United Nations in 1965, was China's greatest diplomatic triumph, and Indonesia's return a year later was China's greatest defeat. The continuing United States policy of blocking an invitation to Peking has only served to obscure the Chinese attitude and to compound the whole problem of the two Chinas and their place in the United Nations.

While the great powers play the leading roles in the diplomatic scene, the supporting cast of middle-sized and small states (especially the new states) both gives to and takes from the stability of the organization. Several nonaligned, small European nations have given yeoman service to the cause of disinterested diplomatic service, and have backed up their service with generous contributions of money and troops. Among these are Sweden, Iceland, Austria, Ireland and, in spite of its own lack of membership, Switzerland. A similar group exists among the small, aligned nations: Canada, Norway and Denmark. Yugoslavia, in addition to providing peacekeeping services, has provided valuable assistance to the developing nations of Africa and Asia without imperial overtones.

The great question is the part that can be played and is being played by the so-called developing nations. For many of these countries, the United Nations has played the role of midwife. It has assisted in the coming of age of former Trust Territories, and has influenced the policies of former colonial powers toward their former colonies. The role that the United Nations has played has resulted in one of the swiftest and most sweeping revolutions in the world's history, involving nearly two billion people.

The impact of this revolution on a United Nations that was already struggling with a somewhat unworkable charter has been tremendous. To the familiar theme of the struggle between the great powers, the revolution has added a fugue of counterstruggle between the "have" and "have-not" nations in which the possibilities for good and evil have been tremendously magnified.

Two elements unite all the developing nations: the desire for complete independence from all colonial or neocolonial political restraints, and the just demand for the correction of the imbalance in economic and technological resources. The first is emotionally explosive, but the latter

101

has no easy short-term solution and demands the special attention of the Christian world, especially the Protestant mercantile world. The United Nations is playing and must play a vital role in international research, planning consultations and activities. Note that the emphasis is international; the situation does not call for a "Big Daddy" but rather for a willingness of all the "have" nations to work with one another and with the "have-nots," who have the responsibility to put their conflicting political and economic demands in some kind of order.

But the United Nations efforts in these directions (notably the Development Program: UNDP; the Trade and Development Conference: UNCTAD; the Industrial Development Organization: UNIDO; and the Specialized Agencies) amount to only about a half a billion dollars annually, an amount equaled by what the United States spends for its Department of Labor, or for the purchase of four nuclear submarines. The United States spends considerably more than this simply for family housing for its military personnel, or for the Federal Aviation Agency. These comparisons show the very limited scale of United Nations resources and the meager size of the great powers' commitment to the United Nations.

The United Nations is not the only international organization. There are military, political and economic regional organizations that play similar roles on a more restricted stage. The formation of military organizations was an early recognition of the impotence of the United Nations as a peace-enforcing instrument in the face of great power confrontation. The North Atlantic Treaty Organization (NATO) was built on this understanding, coinciding as it did with the 1948 abandonment of any serious attempt to make the Military Staff Committee work. With this abandonment the whole idea of an international police force along the lines of the United Nations charter was discarded.

After NATO came the Warsaw Pact, and after that the Dulles sponsored series of "containment" alliances: CENTO (Central Treaty Organization), SEATO (Southeast Asia Treaty Organization), ANZUS (Australia, New Zealand and the United States) and others, and with them the whole concept of aligned and nonaligned nations. While the military organizations are not famous for their contributions to reconciliation, most of them have participated in peacekeeping activities, for example: NATO in Cyprus; the Organization of American States in the Dominican Republic; the Organization of African Unity in the Morocco-Algeria crisis and in the civil wars in the Congo and in Nigeria.

The economic intergovernmental organizations have been more successful, particularly in Europe (the Common Market) and in Latin America. These organizations usually collaborate with the United Nations regional economic commissions. The big question is how flexible they can remain, especially when they are called upon to cooperate in programs that exceed regional boundaries. A hopeful sign in this area has been the formation of a permanent link between the General Agreement on Tariffs and Trade (in which the North Atlantic countries predominate), and UNCTAD (which has become a forum for the poorer Southern nations) in a trade center, to help both developed and developing nations in their trade and tariff problems.

There are a wide variety of nongovernmental international organizations. It is reasonable to say that the more professional and technologically oriented the organization, the less subject it is to chauvinistic and national influences. Therefore, it is usually more willing to contribute valuable services. Examples are: the International Cooperative Alliance, the World Federation of United Nations Associations and the Society for International Development. Without the active support of these highly professional groups, it would be hard to recruit competent technical assistance experts for internationally or nationally supported projects. The specialized agencies of the United Nations are particularly dependent on this kind of support.

In the highly significant field of human rights the world owes much to the support of religious and cultural bodies. The United Nations High Commissioner for Refugees has been able to devote most of his time and meager budget to coordination and direction, while materials, cash and

ield work have been largely supplied by a variety
of private international organizations. The voice
of the nongovernmental organizations has been of
great value at the United Nations itself in the
Economic and Social Council and its commissions.
They suffered serious damage, however, as a result of the revelation of the use (consciously or
unconsciously) of C.I.A. funds by several nongovernmental organizations in the United States.
Their integrity as private organizations has been
seriously damaged.

The technological revolution daily brings all
the nations of the world closer together, whether
it is by the cutting of an hour's time from a trans-
atlantic flight, or five minutes from the delivery
time of a nuclear warhead, by Telstar or by a du-
plicating machine, by the Pill or by disease-re-
sistant rice, by atomic energy or by harvests from
the sea. We must live together or else we will die
together.

Today the possibilities of the latter seem to be
stronger than those of the former. To correct this
imbalance, some form of international organization must exist. If the United Nations had
collapsed under the weight of the many serious
crises that it has survived, some replacement
would have to have been created—unless, of
course, the bomb had been dropped. But the
United Nations has persisted. It is weak. It is
structurally imperfect. It is financially undernourished. But it remains, suffering not so much because of its enemies but because of its friends:

105

the Soviets, who want to lead it into the paths of true Communist virtue; the United States, who wants to be its Great White Father; France, who wants it to reflect the glory of France; Britain who wants it to represent the proven wisdom of the British in dealing with strange people. These may be caricatures of attitudes, but the position can be traced all the way down to its root: nationalism.

The answer for the Christian is that Christ died for all men. The answer for Christian Americans, or Christians of any nationality, is that it is their country's approach to the responsibilities of their membership in the United Nations that counts; attempts to tie the United Nations to their country's coattails is not the answer. Obviously there can be no progress toward an ultimate idea of world government unless there is a parallel movement toward world law.

The record of the International Court of Justice offers very little encouragement here. In the first place, the sweeping restrictions of its authority by the great powers confine its usefulness in any critical situation; in the second place, its advisory opinions on constitutional issues are not binding and have been ignored (e.g., by South Africa in reference to Southwest Africa; by the Soviets in reference to peacekeeping assessments); in the third place, it tends to resort to legal niceties to avoid decisions in a highly charged political situation (Ethiopia and Liberia vs. South Africa); in the fourth place, some nations do not

106

comply with its decisions (Albania), a situation that can only be remedied by resort to the Security Council. Such an action would throw a judicial decision back into the political arena.

But the International Law Commission has made progress in the immense task of codification, including the calling of international conferences (Law of the Sea, Law of Treaty, Law of Consular and Diplomatic Privileges). But the crux of the problem cannot be more clearly illustrated than by the reluctance of the United States to ratify even the most innocuous of human rights treaties. The fear of losing national sovereignty, of being put under legal obligation to heed the complaints of extra-national bodies still prevails. Yet it is only by long, slow steps that a world rule of law can be built.

The key to a rule of law lies in the question of enforcement, and here the slow progress towards disarmament reflects its development. The United Nations can only claim good marks for persistence. Its members have consistently and frequently unanimously confirmed the goal of disarmament, but their actions at the negotiating table belie their words: it is always other nations who must disarm first, who must yield their most advantageous weapons. The ultimate in yielding sovereignty is the yielding of any part of the strength of a good striking arm.

The organ of the United Nations that has the most significant moral force is the Secretariat, embodied in the person of the Secretary General.

107

Much has been written about the conflict between the General Assembly and the Security Council. But it has been the conflict between the Security Council and the Secretary General that has illustrated the dramatic clash between the basic idealism of the charter and the temptation to compromise it by giving preference to national or group self-interest.

It was not simply that the Soviet Union took aggressive measures to downgrade and remove the first two Secretary Generals, and to try to replace one man with a troika. Resistance to the initiative of the office has come from many quarters. Regardless of whether Khrushchev was right when he said that there ". . . could be no neutral man," the truth remains that the position is not tied to group interests and has been better able than any other part of the United Nations to represent the ideals around which the United Nations was created and for which it still survives. The Secretary General is in a position to suggest and assume authority: Mr. Trygve Lie pointed a way in his action in 1950 on the question of the representation of China; Mr. Hammarskjold assumed the necessary authority to make the improvised peacekeeping forces work, and provided far-sighted leadership in the development of resources to face the impending clash between the "have" nations and the "have-not" nations. U Thant continued that leadership and maintained the prestige of the office.

The Secretariat behind the Secretary General

deserves more attention than it usually gets. The whole worldwide force of international civil servants, including the staffs of the specialized agencies and other related organizations, professional and nonprofessional, adds up to a total of 34,000. This is equivalent to the New York City police force, or to the staff of almost every executive department of the United States Government.

In spite of the inevitable snafus of all bureaucracies, in this case complicated by multinational and multilingual factors, the Secretariat has maintained high morale and has shouldered its responsibilities with considerable success. The multireligious factor in its composition is almost completely submerged. I remember an incident in 1948, when as editor of the *Secretariat News* I was trying to get a Christmas message from the Secretary General who happened to be in Paris. The deadline was upon me. I called a friend in the Secretary General's office, explained the situation, and urged him to write one himself. He demurred. "Oh, anyone can write a Christmas message," I said. He replied, "As a practicing Buddhist, I find it quite difficult." (In defense of my insensitivity, let me say that while I knew he was a Thai citizen, he was the chairman of the Oxford-Cambridge Club and occidental in almost every way!)

Behind the structures are the diplomatic skills of national representatives who are capable and willing to work as mediators, go-betweens and negotiators on a completely disinterested basis.

These are the presidents of the Assembly, the chairmen of committees and the heads of essential working groups, who have done effective and unselfish work in a variety of critical situations.

The tremendous importance of the United Nations headquarters site has also been underrated. Its location serves as a means of rapid intercommunication, and is in itself a human community with the personal values of day to day contact. There is a degree of camaraderie that cuts across all political and ideological boundaries. This camaraderie often changes the way in which policies are carried out and it sets a tone for resolving difficult conflicts. Occasionally this irreducibly human dimension breaks through to the surface. At the conclusion of Security Council debate on the Non-Proliferation Treaty on June 19, 1968, and after long and tedious discussion and bargaining in many parts of the world, the United Kingdom's Lord Caradon paid warm and witty tribute to his American and Russian colleagues.

To Ambassador Arthur Goldberg, he said:

Winston Churchill used to say that he was half American and all English. You, Sir, can do better than that. You have Ambassador Berard's testimony on Monday that you have the mind of a Frenchman. Ambassador Eralp told us yesterday that you have the will of a Turk. I hesitate to attribute to you any additional national characteristics. Certainly you have a mastery of politics, which we have all learned from the Greeks. We have also good

reason to know that you have something of the
obstinacy which is a characteristic common, I
like to think, to the Russians and the British.
So, if we are to believe all that is said of you,
we must conclude that you are some kind of
international monstrosity. We content ourselves
with thinking that, whatever characteristics of
other nations you may have, you are certainly
all American.

Then to the Soviet spokesman, Lord Caradon
said:

I would also wish to say a word to Deputy
Foreign Minister Kuznetsov, who, I understand,
will be returning very soon to his great country.
We are always glad to see him. When he comes
we confidently expect agreement, and we expect
action. We are never disappointed. Deputy
Foreign Minister Kuznetsov and Ambassador
Malik make a formidable team, and we greatly
respect them.

As I have sat here in the council, I have oc-
cupied myself by composing these memorable
lines which I dedicate to the Deputy Foreign
Minister:

When prospects are dark and hopes are dim,
We know that we must send for him;
When storms and tempests fill the sky,
"Bring on Kuznetsov," is the cry.

He comes like a dove from the Communist ark,
And light appears where all was dark;
His coming quickly turns the tide,
The propaganda floods subside.

And now that he has changed the weather,
Lion and lamb can vote together.
God bless the Russian delegation.
I waive consecutive translation.

The sometimes derided United Nations cocktail parties have a value all their own, and to most of their participants represent work rather than play. The presence of the world's press and other communications media, and the representatives of both international and national nongovernmental organizations, make the parties invaluable assets to greater understanding.

What can the churches contribute to this international body? Each of the great religions of the world declares the gospel of the good neighbor; all the signatories of the charter subscribe to it. Admittedly the United Nations' peacekeeping efforts have been in the area of workable crisis expediencies and have not led to permanent peace. By the same token, its much greater contributions in peacebuilding, in the areas of human rights, economic equity and social justice, have made slow progress and have attracted minimal financial support. Disarmament lags behind arming, and the rule of law is far away.

Yet the need and the hope remain. A churchman seems to be faced with two tasks. One is to exert what influence he can muster on his government's policies and the opinion of his fellow countrymen on matters of foreign policy and international interdependence. He can help bring understanding that the United Nations is the one existing piece of machinery whereby international understanding and cooperation can most effectively take place, and that it cannot be judged solely on the basis of what it is doing for any particular nation. The other task is for the churchman to develop contacts and understanding between religions all over the world, who recognize the basic principles of the charter and are willing under reasonable conditions to encourage their own governments to use the alternatives that the United Nations provides to a steady march to Armageddon. The proof of ecumenicity lies in mutual faith and understanding.

Chapter 5
Alan Geyer

Apostles of Conflict and Agents of Reconciliation

The maze of peace is a labyrinth of human conflicts that can never be fully resolved. This could seem to be a terribly pessimistic view of our world. There is indeed, as all the authors of these pages testify, a dense thicket of ideological, political, economic, racial, legal and religious obstacles to the realization of the world's dream of peace.

But conflict is not always and everywhere a Bad Thing. Conflict is the source of vitality and creativity in all human beings and communities. Without conflict, you would be dead. Without conflict, a government is stifled, an economy suffocates, a religion dies. Conflict is inevitable and necessary. Conflict is the precious gift of a gracious God. Conflict testifies to the freedom of all the children of God.

Yet conflict can also become the perversion of freedom and the destroyer of life itself. It can be a crippler of the mind and a corrupter of the spirit. It can kill the world.

Both conflict and the absence of conflict can be the enemies of humanity.

Reconciliation is not the repression of conflict but rather the redemption of conflict. Reconciliation accepts conflict as a given, and works through it to prepare men to receive the gift of peace. Whatever the social outcome of human struggle, there is a peace that this world can neither give nor take away. It is the peace that is given to those who have struggled, sacrificed and suffered for humanity itself. Humanity is not an abstraction for the Christian: it is the image of Christ in every man and in the depths of one's own being. It is as concrete and as vivid as torn flesh and flowing blood.

The world and the church shy away from the miracle of reconciliation because they do not or will not understand the dimensions of conflict in all its promise and peril.

What if this were not so? What if Christians were to become the apostles of conflict so that they could become authentic agents of reconciliation?

These things would happen:

1. *The apostles of conflict would take the long and the large view of peace.* They would not expect the struggle for peace to be finished in a year or ten years or a lifetime. Even if they rally to such a slogan as PEACE NOW! to express their protest against the war policies of their governments, they know that the human race is en-

gaged in what the late President Kennedy called a "long twilight struggle."

Americans have a special fondness for crusades and crash programs, for the notion that an all-out but short-term effort will solve basic problems. The churches of America have repeatedly sought through their crusades, "emphases," "priority programs" and "challenges" to do what in the real world simply cannot be done. Impatience can be a source of moral energy and renewed dedication but it can also be a sign of immaturity and superficial commitment. Beware of all kinds of crash programs and panaceas on the peace front!

A gracious and competent Catholic economist, Barbara Ward, who as a Britisher is also one of our most useful friendly critics, has pointed out this American addiction to crash programs as a troublesome feature in our relations with the rest of the world. Cultural differences are too great and the problems to be confronted are too stubborn for a brief burst of effort. "A crash program," she says, "is like a man having an affair with nine women simultaneously, hoping to produce an offspring in just one month. It just can't be done!"

As urgent as a political settlement of the war in Vietnam has become, it is equally important to prevent future Vietnams. Vietnam is not just an isolated event. On the larger scene, Vietnam is a symptom, a revelation of many other problems and attitudes. Vietnam is a revelation of our faulty assumptions about China, of the shortcomings of our grasp of economic aid, of the limits of military power, of our distorted view of nationalistic revolutions, of the poverty of our political philosophy and of the grotesque imbalance in our national priorities.

The long and the large view of peace means getting beyond the trap of reacting to crises only after they have exploded in violence and suffering. It means having a notion of *preventive policy*. At this writing, it would suggest the following:

a. *The problem of human coexistence between China and the United States* looms ahead as a dimension of every other international problem. The study of Chinese language and culture in public schools, as well as a patient and determined effort to open up exchange programs between Chinese and Americans, may be as important a project for peace as any that can be imagined.

b. *The problem of systematic poverty* in the less developed countries and in the international economic system is the overriding issue of justice that cuts across the issues of war and peace. The understanding of this new world of international economic interdependence and its racial implications is a radical challenge to the churches and to United States policy in matters of trade, aid, investment and currency.

c. *The problem of security and arms control* calls for sustained citizen attention and action if the arms race is to be reversed, the nation's resources redirected to the alleviation of poverty at home and abroad, and the structures of common security strengthened among nations.

117

China, international development, arms control and security: these are the three long range challenges that should loom largest in Christian strategy and United States concern. They may not seem dramatic enough to some of today's peaceniks or politicians, but to neglect them today will guarantee a tide of tragedy tomorrow.

2. *The apostles of conflict would become politically engaged.* Every great issue of justice and of human fulfillment has become a *political* issue in our generation. Many Christians are notoriously unable to face up to the inescapable fact of politics. They are even incapable of defining "politics" as a word: it is disdained as a sordid activity for the unrighteous. But politics, rightly understood, is the struggle for power and purpose in all human communities. The Christian (or the church) who pretends to be nonpolitical is pretending his way into indifference to the human condition in our time.

Peace is not nonpolitical. It is possible to have a full schedule of programs related to peace—filmstrips, field trips, study groups—which never get at the substance of controversy or conflict, and which never relate people effectively to the structures of power that determine the outcome of the quest for peace. Even social action leaders try to find nonpolitical escapes from public controversy. And having remained outside the political process, they flail about in some new crises looking for instant influence and are unable to find it. Politics requires a vocational commitment through

118

the months and years of pulling and hauling and willing and losing. This is the way that someone earns the right to be influential in the world.

Commenting on the inescapably political demands of the presidency, Harry Truman once warned: "If you can't stand the heat, you'd better get out of the kitchen!" Political involvement for churches or for individuals tends to turn the heat on. But there is no more important aspect of the ministry of reconciliation than for the churches to nurture their people in the faith and skills that enable them to accept and redeem controversy. The filmstrip and field trip approach to peace will not do that, although such things may serve as practical aids. If we are serious about affirming our need for "courage in the struggle for justice and peace" (according to a modern creed), we shall not become desperately preoccupied with every sweet, safe, noncontroversial, nonpolitical means to win that struggle.

There is a beautiful Hebrew word for peace: *shalom*. It is a word that suggests the radiance and wholeness of peace in every dimension of life as a gift of God. An experimental Christian group in the Netherlands has taken this word for its own name. A recent paper published by the group called for *politicians of shalom* to become engaged in the battle for world economic justice:

> Politicians of shalom. That means: peace on earth among men who are of this political goodwill. We do not lack ideas, expertise, mechanisms or money. We lack the political will to

119

put these to the well-being of the inhabited world.

Take these words and try them on for size. Are you willing to become a *politician of shalom?*

3. *The apostles of conflict would dare to challenge the policies, priorities and assumptions of their own government.* Respect for the heritage of a nation and the heavy burdens of its government is fundamental to any adequate Christian approach to citizenship. Too many morally aroused people have little appreciation for the complexities of public responsibility: they are impulsively antigovernmental. But respect for government is dangerous when it becomes reverence, when it exalts the institutions of government above the human rights of the people to be served by government. The political thinkers of the eighteenth century gave us the sharp warning that human rights are the rightful masters of government, not government the master of human rights. This remains a permanently revolutionary doctrine.

In recent years we have witnessed the consolidation of economic wealth, military strategy and political institutions into a new governmental system that might be called "military socialism." We cling desperately to the myths of a market economy based on free enterprise. In fact, our ideological rhetoric frequently puts the myths of the market in the highest place in the hierarchy of sacred things that are at stake in the cold war.

Yet our continuing existence as a warfare state (which is really more to the point than "welfare state"!) has entangled defense policy and institutions in industrial development, labor-management relations, education, science, journalism, civil liberties and almost every other realm of our national life. The fact that more than half of the national budget is allocated to defense and related areas has fostered an immense defense lobby with billions of dollars at stake. Congressmen, generals, scientists and corporation magnates are all mixed up in the action.

Ideologically we have repudiated socialism and all its works. Existentially we are experiencing a degree of socialism far in advance of many nations who openly embrace the name of socialism.

Effective action for peace cannot escape the fact of military socialism. (President Eisenhower called it "the military-industrial complex" in his farewell message.) There is a scramble for national priorities among a people who have rather suddenly discovered that they cannot do everything. It is a contest that is taking place within the structures of military socialism. Hard choices have to be made that involve not only military strategy as such but also the allocation of limited resources either in new offensive and defensive missile systems and space spectaculars or in the reconstruction of our cities and aid to the less developed countries.

New forms of ministry, study and political

action are required if the churches are not to continue to be irrelevant to the structures of decision making. Christians must not forfeit the capacity to wage conflict when human rights are being ground up in the machinery of military socialism.

4. *The apostles of conflict would lead in the transformation of the mission of the church from charity to justice.* The world mission of the church, as Dr. Kitagawa has pointed out, is still maintained essentially as an enterprise of charity. Even though many mission leaders are aware of this, they help to perpetuate structures that are heavy-laden with Victorian paternalism, preoccupied with relief rather than reconstruction and development, concerned with the church's own marginal projects rather than with the overriding issues of public policy, busy with the operations of philanthropy rather than with witness in the world of politics. In a similar way, the energies and resources of Christian education are preoccupied with church school programs to the neglect of the issues of justice in the vastly more important systems of public education.

To turn from charity to justice means, in a sense, to turn the church inside out. It is to transcend the isolationism of individual and local life to engage the systems of human interdependence in the world. It is to conceive of *systems ministries* in such seemingly obscure realms as military technology, international trade and communications media.

Some young poeple and youth leaders have

recently announced a "guerrilla war" against "the whole mission-service establishment" of the churches in order to dramatize the claims of justice against the projects of charity. They have focused on the issue of international trade, especially in regard to the exploitation of the poor nations by the rich nations. They are daring to propose that this is the most critical matter confronting the world church!

5. *The apostles of conflict would know that they need to be on the receiving as well as the sending end of missions.* One of the prices we have paid for the wealth of the American nation is having a one-way relationship to the work of Christianity around the world. We don't know what it is like to be the target of missions. Too often American political and cultural ideas have gotten all mixed up with the Christian message that our missionaries have taken to other lands. We have not experienced within the life of our churches the challenge to these ideas that can only come from Christians of other nations and cultures. This is especially true in regard to Christians in the new nations, their perspectives on the meaning of their faith for peace, justice, revolution and encounter with other religions.

We must make room in our church programs for missionaries from many other countries of the world. They might preach a gospel that is painful for us to hear—but which might save us. A new appreciation of the values of *intentional conflict* is essential to world missions.

Envoys of Mankind

Apostles of conflict must know, of course, that conflict is not the ultimate fact about man.

The maze of peace could overwhelm us with its complexity. Such is the multiplicity of human conflicts that even if we become actively engaged in trying to resolve them we can get sidetracked or lost.

But every once in a while someone comes along and cuts through the maze. Our sharpness of purpose and sense of direction are restored. The message of reconciliation is brought to a clear historical focus. There was such a moment in October, 1965, when an Italian Catholic, Pope Paul VI, came to the United Nations General Assembly. With impassioned eloquence, he cried to the delegates of the nations:

> Listen to the lucid words of the great departed John Kennedy, who proclaimed, four years ago: "Mankind must put an end to war, or war will put an end to mankind."
>
> Many words are not needed to proclaim this loftiest aim of your institution. It suffices to remember that the blood of millions of men, that numberless and unheard of sufferings, useless slaughter and frightful ruin, are the sanction of the pact that unites you, with an oath that must change the future history of the world: *no more war, war never again!* Peace. It is peace which must guide the destinies of peoples and of all mankind. . . .
>
> The hour has struck for our "conversion,"

for personal transformation, for interior re-
newal. We must get used to thinking of man
in a new way; and in a new way also of man's
life in common; with a new manner, too, of
conceiving the paths of history and the destiny
of the world. . . .

The hour has struck for a halt, a moment of
recollection, of reflection, almost of prayer. A
moment to think anew of our common origin,
our history, our common destiny.

Technology has created some new symbols of
hope for such a moment as this. The United Nations General Assembly has framed a Declaration of Legal Principles having to do with international cooperation in space. The ninth of these
principles elevates astronauts to a new status unprecedented in international law: "States shall
regard astronauts as envoys of mankind, and shall
render them all possible assistance in the event
they have an accident, suffer distress, or make an
emergency landing."

"Envoys of mankind"—a legal principle—but
what a principle for Christian faith and life in
these revolutionary times!

Envoys of mankind.

Politicians of shalom.

Apostles of conflict.

Agents of reconciliation.

Notes

Chapter 1

1. G.H.C. MacGregor, *The New Testament Basis of Pacifism* (New York: The Fellowship of Reconciliation, 1936), p. 7.
2. Richard Hofstadter, *Anti-Intellectualism in American Life* (New York: Random House, 1966).
3. Richard Shaull, "Revolutionary Change in Theological Perspective," in John C. Bennett (ed.), *Christian Social Ethics in a Changing World* (New York: Association Press, 1966), p. 26.
4. André Trocmé, *The Politics of Repentance* (New York: Fellowship Publications, 1953).
5. Herbert H. Farmer, *God and Man* (New York: Abingdon-Cokesbury Press, 1947), p. 190.

Chapter 2

1. Carl Oglesby and Richard Shaull, *Containment and Change* (New York: Macmillan, 1967), p. 213.
2. Quoted by Walter Feurich in "Wir sind in die irre gegangen." *Neue Zeit,* August 5, 1967.
3. *Constitution on the Church in the Modern World,* Second Vatican Council, Dec. 7, 1965, publ. by National Catholic Welfare Conference, p. 88.
4. Roger Garaudy, *From Anathema to Dialogue, A Marxist Challenge to the Christian Churches* (New York: Herder and Herder, 1966), p. 31.
5. Karl Marx, "Contribution to the Critique of Hegel's Philosophy of Right," 1844, quoted by Herbert Apthekar in *Political Affairs,* July ,1966.
6. John C. Bennett, "Changes in the Communist World," *Concern,* Board of Social Concerns of the Methodist Church, Sept. 1, 1965.
7. Raul P. Prebisch, Church and Society Conference, Geneva, 1966, quoted in *The Development Apocalypse,* a Risk paperback, 1 & 2, 1967, p. 55.
8. Paul Albrecht, Department of Church and Society, World Council of Churches.
9. Roger Garaudy, *op. cit.,* p. 31.
10. Josef L. Hromadka, "The Ethics of Revolution," transcript of an address given at the Conference on the Ethics of Revolution held at Boston University, Nov. 19, 1966.

11. *World Conference on Church and Society: Official Report* (Geneva: World Council of Churches, 1967).
12. Quoted in "Nationalism," Encyclopedia Britannica, 1959, Vol. 16, p. 150.
13. "Die Lage der Vertriebenen und das Verhaeltnis des deutschen Volkes zu seinen oestlichen Nachbarn," (Hannover: 1965), p. 29. Tr. by Christoph Schmauch.
14. Colin W. Williams, *For the World* (New York: National Council of Churches, 1965), p. 46.
15. *International Review of Missions*, July, 1967, p. 340.
16. Thich Nhat Hanh, *Vietnam: Lotus in a Sea of Fire* (New York: Hill and Wang, 1967), p. ix.
17. *Ibid.*, p. 25.

Chapter 3

1. W. E. B. Du Bois, *The Souls of Black Folk*, 1903, Chapter 2, "Of the Dawn of Freedom".
2. Among others, see Ronald Segal, *The Race War* (New York: Viking Press, 1967; also as a paperback, Bantam Books).
3. See C. Eric Lincoln, *The Black Muslims in America*, the first authoritative study of this movement (Boston: Beacon Press, 1961).
4. On this point documentation is hardly necessary, but a few books may be listed:
   Charles E. Silberman, *Crisis in Black and White*, (New York: Random House, 1964). Lerone Bennett, Jr., *The Negro Mood* (New York: Ballantine Books, 1964). E. U. Essien-Udom, *Black Nationalism: A Search for an Identity in America*, (Chicago: University of Chicago Press, 1962; New York: Dell Publishing Co., Laurel Edition, 1964). Stokely Carmichael and Charles V. Hamilton, *Black Power: The Politics of Liberation in America* (New York: Vintage Books, 1967). Charles E. Fager, *White Reflections on Black Power*, (Eerdmans, 1967).
5. George Padmore, *Pan-Africanism or Communism?* (London: Dobson Books, 1955).
6. George Balandier, "Negritude," in Hughes and Thompson, *Race: Individual and Collective Behavior* (New York: The Free Press, 1958). Franz Fanon, *Black Skin, White Masks*, tr. by Charles L. Markmann (New York: Grove Press, 1967). Originally *Peau Noire, Masques Blancs* (Paris, 1952).
7. Jan-heinz Jahn, *Muntu: An Outline of Neo-African Culture* (New York: Grove Press). Victor C. Ferkiss,

Africa's Search for Identity (New York: George Braziller, 1966).

8. See among others, Edwin O. Reischauer, *Beyond Vietnam: The United States and Asia,* (New York: Vintage Books, 1967), pp. 60-64.

9. See *World Conference on Church and Society: Official Report* (Geneva: World Council of Churches, 1967). For a popular but authoritative account of this extremely important conference see: J. Brooke Mosley, *Christians in the Technical and Social Revolutions of Our Time* (Cincinnati: Forward Movement Publications, paperback, 1966).

10. Edwin O. Reischauer, *op. cit.,* pp. 46-52.

11. Robert Heilbroner, *The Future as History* (New York: Harper & Row, 1960), p. 162.

12. Geoffrey Barraclough, *An Introduction to Contemporary History* (New York: Hillary, 1965), pp. 104, 119.

13. Ronald Segal, *op. cit.,* p. viii.

14. Nathan Wright, *Black Power and Urban Unrest: Creative Possibilities* (New York: Hawthorn Books, 1967), pp. 66 ff.

15. See "White Power: The Colonial Situation," in Carmichael and Hamilton, *Black Power;* also Fanon, *op. cit.* and his *The Wretched of the Earth* (New York: Grove Press, paperback, 1966).

16. Carmichael and Hamilton, *op. cit.*

17. See Stan Steiner, *The New Indians* (New York: Harper and Row, 1968.

18. Charles Fager, *op. cit.*

19. Edwin O. Reischauer, *op. cit.,* pp. 47-52.

20. *Ibid.,* p. 52.

21. *World Conference on Church and Society: Official Report* (Geneva: World Council of Churches, 1967).

22. Franz Fanon, *The Wretched of the Earth,* p. 76.

23. Robert Heilbroner, *The Great Ascent: The Struggle for Economic Development in Our Time* (New York: Harper & Row, 1963), p. 104.

24. *What Is a Jew?—a Reader,* compiled and edited by Solomon S. Bernards (New York: Anti-Defamation League of B'nai Brith), pp. 9-10.

377-09211-8

$1.45

ABOUT THE AUTHORS

ALAN GEYER
has been at work on international relations as chairman of the political science department at Mary Baldwin College, as staff member of the Council for Christian Social Action of the United Church of Christ, as an author and as recently-appointed editor of the **Christian Century. Piety and Politics: American Protestantism in the World Arena** came from his pen in 1963.

CHRISTOPH SCHMAUCH
works on world scene as part-time staff member for the United Methodists at the Church Center for the United Nations. He is also an officer of the Christian Peace Conference and pastor of a church.

DAISUKE KITAGAWA
maintains a world-wide network of relationships as a staff member of the Division of World Mission and Evangelism of the World Council of Churches, Geneva, Switzerland.

GERARD N. T. WIDDRINGTON
is constantly at work interpreting the United Nations and its activities both to groups coming to the Church Center for the United Nations and through his staff work in the Department of International Relations of the National Council of Churches.

FRIENDSHIP PRESS • NEW YORK